EARLY

THE ESOTERIC

"This bold and groundbreaking new book takes the whole human race forward by a step. Maha and David Pan Brown have created a highly enjoyable instruction manual for the development of enlightened relationships, and thereby bravely led us all towards a New Paradigm for marriage, one focused on the Divine Self and based on the highest spiritual truths. Beautifully written, and full of wise advice on all aspects of developing a healthy, spiritually in-tune relationship, this book is the perfect gift for all aspiring to let their marriage become a path to awakening. The scope and detail in the steps they offer us are remarkable, and show a rare level of wisdom, harmonized with compassion and emotional integration. This is a book to treasure, and to read again and again as the years go by. Heartily recommended for all on the path of the Heart!"
- Ram Das Batchelder, Author of Rising in Love

"This book could be the best guidance there is for learning to walk the spiritual path within relationship. It has the potency to protect the couple from obstacles and help them to proceed on the path of Peace. I have no doubt this work will succeed in sowing fresh seeds for fortunate future rebirths and attainments of full Enlightenment by all its readers." *- Venerable Lama Ngwang Rigzdin, Founder of the Nepal Reiki & Meditation Center*

"This book points the reader towards a non-dual awareness and awakening to oneness in a very beautiful and practical way! Coming from an experience of the teachings of *A Course in Miracles* it resonates deeply to read about how meditation and forgiveness is shared practically with deep integrity and acknowledgement of the truth of one another's being. We feel that The Esoteric Path of Marriage is a unique and truly helpful book for couples in spiritual awakening!" *- Jenny and Greg Donner, Living Miracles Europe*

"The Browns have unveiled an elegant guide, illuminating the path to enlightened relationship. A must read for anyone interested in a deep and soulful union." *- Joseph D Drumheller - Author of the award winning novel, The Unity Oracle*

"A wonderful guide on spiritual evolution in partnership that transcends common habitual and dis-empowering perspectives on relationships in society, providing good examples and better choices to make in the most key challenging times." *– Roman Hanis, Director of Indigenous Healing Center, Paititi Institute*

"The book does a great job of explaining the key attributes of a successful relationship which is focused on maximizing the personal spiritual growth of each member of the relationship, as well as assisting each person to function from essence, rather than from ego. It is a great book for those contemplating marriage, as well as for those who feel their marriage has hit a proverbial wall or if not serving the higher purpose of both partners." *- Diadra & John A. Price (Co-Authors of Soular Reunion: Journey to the Beloved - Re-Membering the Love of Self, Soulmates & Twin Souls)*

"The deeper we go into exploring what sacred relationship and marriage means and consciously approach it as an every-moment spiritual practice, the more all tiny parts of our pain-body start presenting themselves with all their deeply encoded contractions asking (sometimes crying) for the LOVE they haven't received. Maha and David's book is an excellent read to guide and remind us of this profound process and most of all of our commitment to Truth. I highly recommend this beautiful and intimate book to all." *- Arpita Hackenberg, co-founder of Mahadevi Ashram, Guatemala*

The Esoteric Path *of* Marriage

www.esotericpathofmarriage.com

The Esoteric Path

*of M*arriage

A Guide To Spiritual Enlightenment

Through Relationship

MAHA BROWN

&

DAVID PAN BROWN

Sacred Human Press

Sacred Human Press

www.sacredhumanpress.com

ISBN: 9780692633748
ISBN-13: 978-0-692-63374-8

DEDICATION

Dedicated to the One Eternal, Living Presence;
Our Beloved and Great Teacher

CONTENTS

PREFACE xiii

AFFIRMATION FOR FREEDOM xiii

SPECIAL THANKS xvii

1   **THE ESOTERIC PATH OF MARRIAGE**   **1**
The Purpose of this Book   3
From Head to Heart   7
Marriage in the Old Paradigm   10
The New Paradigm   11
Relationship in the New Paradigm   12

2   **EMERGING FROM MILLENNIA OF**   **13**
    PATRIARCHY
How Patriarchy Came About   13
What Becomes of Woman in   14
Patriarchy?
What Becomes of Man in Patriarchy?   16
Attraction   17

Respect for Child   19
Relationship Dynamic of the Old   21
Paradigm

**3   AGREEMENTS OF THE ESOTERIC PATH   25
     OF MARRIAGE**
The Fourteen Agreements of the   27-44
Esoteric Path of Marriage

**4   PASHA ON THE PATH OF   45
     PARTNERSHIP**
Looking Through the Eyes of Others   46
Speaking Ill of Your Partner   47
Keeping Score   48
Compare and Despair   48
Martyrdom   49
Attachment   50
Jealousy   53
Indulging in Woe-is-Us Mentality   56
Pushing a Reluctant Partner   57

**5   THE FALSE SELF AND THE PLAY OF   59
     CREATION**
The Origins of Ego   59
The Building of the False Self   67
Personality Traits of the False Self   71
Characteristics of the True Self   80

6   SLAYING THE DRAGON   81
The Elephant in the Room   81
Make Space to Feel   84
Drop the Story   85
Transcend Ordinary Negativity   86
The Marital Pain-body   87

It's Just Pain Talking   88
Transmuting a Difference of Opinion   89
Healing Acute Conflict   91
Conflict Avoidance   93
Healing Anger   93
Managing Extreme Pain-bodies   95
Developing Compassion for Yourself   99
Expanding Your Awareness into the   101
World

7   COMMUNE-ICATION   103
Listening is the Key   103
Speak Your Truth   104
When to Let Pain Speak?   106
Jabbering   108
Address Your Partner's Highest Self   109
"What's Wrong?"   110
Eliminate Control Language   111
Honor Your Awareness   112
Eliminate Unconscious Speech   114
Patterns
Masks & Little White Lies   114
Om Namah Sivaya   115
Banter   117
Treading on Egg Shells?   117
Baby-Talk   118
Pet Names? Make them Conscious!   119
Calling Between Rooms, A Good Idea?   120

8   PRACTICAL WAYS TO PROMOTE   121
    HARMONY AND UNITY
Meditation   121
Healing One Another   126
Time Apart – Accept and Enjoy   128

Soul-Gazing   131
The Big OM   131
Sacred Dance   133
Love-making   134
Diet   135
Take Refuge in Silence   136
Play   137

9   NAVIGATING THE LABYRINTH   139
Money   140
Purpose   144
Materialism   145
In the Fire   146
Environments   148
Prayer   149
Tragedy   150

10   OPENING PANDORA'S BOX   157
SEX AS SADHANA   159
TRANSCENDING THE PERSONAL   177

ACKNOWLEDGEMENTS   183

BIG THANKS   185

GLOSSARY   187

PREFACE

Spiritual teachings often (but not always) come wrapped in words, the same as the juice of a sugar cane has a husk*. Common sense tells us to drink the juice, discarding the husk but all too often people spit out the juice and continue to chew on the fibrous husks.

We offer this book that it may assist the evolution of consciousness on this planet. We invite you to use it as a point of reference to return to as you and your relationships evolve. If you are not currently in a relationship but are open to one, perhaps it will help you to focus your mind to attain the relationship your

---

* The sugar cane metaphor is from Amma (the Hugging Saint).

Heart most desires.

If a practice or teaching doesn't speak to you directly, move on; perhaps it's not for you or will be for you at a later time. Perhaps it will still spark some contemplation inside of you or open up a conversation within your relationship. What is for you now will hit you like an epiphany (an ah-ha!); so very obvious, you'll realize its Truth was with you all along, it just took shining a Light on it to be revealed.

At its best 'spiritual teaching' validates the Wisdom-Understanding within and gives you more faith in your Self.

AFFIRMATION FOR FREEDOM

Your resistance of me keeps you separate from me and I
can't feed that resistance no more.
I'm going back to a place where love grows on trees and
money can't buy you anything.
Back to where birds sing for free
Back to Nature.
Back to living in harmony.
Back to where men are equal as sheep.
Women, equal as jewels.
Back to where the sun shines all day and flows its
reflection from your heart to mine and back again.
Never missing a beat.
Nothing to stumble
and obstacles is not even a word.
Fear has not been formed, neither doubt, nor anger,
and possessions; a concept that's rather absurd.
There is nothing to give. Nothing to own. Life is there
to be lived and live it does.
Effortless.
As a mother loves a child and a child loves and loves to
be loved.
Let us call this place

......and worship and marvel at its wonder.

By David Pan Brown

SPECIAL THANKS

To Barbara for your faith in that place with no name
and holding space for us to get there.

The Esoteric Path

of Marriage

1. THE ESOTERIC PATH OF MARRIAGE

"What is to give light must endure burning."
-Victor E. Frankl

People wonder about us: "What is the secret of their relationship? They are like two moving as one, yet still uniquely themselves."

Or simply, "There's something different going on with those two."

Those on a Spiritual Path often share: "I want a relationship like yours. Before meeting you, I didn't think it possible."

"They must be newly-married," strangers muse.

Yet we have been married for years and some of those years we have spent hardly a moment apart. "They must just be really similar," others suggest.

But no, we are from different backgrounds and different parts of the World, although - Self-Realization - as a primary focus is shared by us both.

"Well, perhaps they just both came from very happy families, with good relationship examples to follow."

Not so, David's father was an alcoholic and his mother lived in fear of him. He killed himself when David was thirteen.

"Well, maybe their relationship has been plain sailing, an easy time of it." People assume.

"Maybe they were so evolved they didn't have much 'stuff' to go through. Maybe they've never fought."

Wrong on all counts, in fact during our time together we have shed many skins and faced many challenges as well as a year of separation due to border control, and even tragedy; we lost a son in childbirth.

So we are not talking about the appearance of happiness or the enjoyment of a particularly agreeable set of life circumstances but a life of (inner and outer) Adventure amid a background-bliss deeper than the ebb and flow of life's events.

We enjoy a dynamic that serves both our Spirits well. A dynamic we *fostered* within our relationship and now enjoy in the World. It is a dynamic that has helped us to awaken spiritually and connect to the source of Life; the I AM Presence; 'the Peace that passeth all understanding' that is the birthright of us all. It is from this place we have anchored our relationship and it is *only* from this place that we can truly begin to Thrive.

So what are the Keys of a relationship that carries the vibration of Joy, Unconditional Love, Bliss and Peace evolving into feelings of Devotion and Unity?

THE PURPOSE OF THIS BOOK

It is our wish to share with those seeking Truth and those seeking truly fulfilling relationship the path that we have blazed; to forge a relationship that will help them to find and dwell in the Peace of what and who they really are.

It is also our wish through this book to update the function of marriage as an institution that served a purpose in the Old Paradigm into a vehicle for transformation as we enter a new paradigm that works for the many and not just for the few. For as old structures fall away we are finding ways to make the World a better place. Clean energy solutions, systems to eradicate hunger and thirst, new technologies to enable us to work together to better the human experience and even help us to explore our solar system. But if we do not find a way to create happy human relations then we cannot live in a happy world.

The New Paradigm is not in the future it is a subtle vibration to enter into in the present moment and this book is in its way a manual to help you to bring your primary relationship into that vibration.

Our journey has been a full-on, passionate, lightening-speed dash towards the Truth, forsaking all else. The intensity of our calling towards Self-Realization has created the most challenging of circumstances on the physical, which we almost completely neglected for some years as we lived on higher dimensions in blissful communion with the Divine. As such we have relied on Divine Providence and with often no safety net but our trust in the process we were in and our faith in and love for the Eternal Presence.

This journey has entailed a shedding of our conditioned selves and has made for a wonderful, if brutal opportunity to bring it all up and either evolve or suffer. We don't see for us we could have done it any other way. So we learned to evolve in the backdrop of the most trying of circumstances as we trust all do.

Thus, this book is for spiritual warriors who are ready to forge an enlightened relationship. A relationship that instead of being a source of pointless suffering, is a source of tremendous growth. A relationship that instead of playing off of the hind-brain, reactionary records of our forbears plays straight from the creative force itself. One that is geared towards our perfection in every pristine moment. At its core this book seeks to assist us to alchemize a relationship that keeps us imprisoned in the Mundane into a vehicle that can, with perseverance and Compassion, elevate us into direct, blissful relationship with the Cosmic Beloved.

Here, we prepare to make our relationship with our partner, our *sadhana*, our spiritual practice. For this book will share the very esoteric, extraordinarily powerful, path of a partnership approach to Waking Up.

If you are reading this book and you don't have a partner, are searching for your partner or have all but given up on the hope of ever having a positive, sustained relationship on the spiritual path, take heart and read on.

Introducing what follows into your psyche will in itself encode you with a vibration, a clarity, and a direction. Whenever we are specific about the divine purpose behind what it is that we want, the Universe conspires on our (Its) behalf. For instance, don't just wish to be in a relationship or even a happy relationship but when you feel ready, request of your deepest self a relationship through which you can enlighten yourself and serve the light of the World. These kinds of prayers that are in harmony with the whole are sure to be answered!

Many prescribe the path of renunciation as the only path to Love without Opposite, however, there is a very narrow path, (call it a super-highway if you like for it can get you where you're going so fast!), where renunciation takes place within a joyful relationship.

Don't get us wrong, this is not a handbook for a happy marriage, this is a guidebook for spiritual growth directed towards union with Self/God/the Substratum *through* marriage. Marriage, in this case, means two that are married, meaning merged in relationship irrespective of any legally binding document.

Perhaps to some seekers amongst you this sounds paradoxical. For by renunciation we mean, renouncing the world of material effects, and marriage seems to necessitate donning the shackles of worldly responsibility so how in the World can we become Free amid that? Dearest Hearts read on and hold on to your hats for The Esoteric Path of Marriage is spiritual rocket fuel!

FROM HEAD TO HEART

Whilst the dynamic is shifting within us, as moment-by-moment we allow the true seat of consciousness in the Heart to lead, and be supported by the mind (instead of entirely run by it) the civilization has a ways to go before it catches up with this inner-revolution, which is happening one Human Being at a time throughout the globe.

This painstaking switch within us of moving the 'power' from head to Heart itself equates to Spiritual Awakening. We are essentially reversing millennia of collective conditioning whilst living amid a dying structure that never-the-less continues to uphold its model and patterning.

There was a recent study (performed by HeartMath) that reveals the profound intelligence of the heart as the seat of consciousness that is connected to That not bound by Time. They studied the flow of information between the heart and the brain. What they discovered was something that surprised them.

The participants in the study were wired up to various sensors to measure their brainwaves, their heartbeats and so on. They were then exposed to a series of images. Some were 'high arousal' like a car crash or a snake striking while others were 'low arousal' like bunny rabbits and nature scenes.

When they analyzed all the data, they found that the heart seemed to *know* the images before the participant ever saw the images with their eyes! If the future picture was going to be one of the emotionally arousing ones the heart rate started to drop around 5 seconds before the image was randomly selected to be shown on the screen. So nobody could know what this future picture was going to be.[1]

This backs up what scientists of consciousness (meditators) have known for millennia, that information runs into the heart first from a field of consciousness that is beyond the physical, then to the brain and then into the body; whereas old paradigm reality does not acknowledge the consciousness of the heart. The brain, as fed by the five senses is seen as the ultimate 'knower'. This leaves out the function of the Heart, essentially cutting man off from the source of creation, connectedness, intelligence and Life itself, which is fed by the elusive sixth sense that is not really elusive at all, it connects everything, through the Heart. Thus operating 'out of Time' as it does, The Heart works at a non-linear level, independent of the physical laws of reality and thus it seems, at a quantum level of reality, processing information at the sub-atom level. So the Heart is the original 'quantum computer', the gateway to the Universal Mind.

---

[1] These results have since been replicated in many different independent labs around the World.

MARRIAGE IN THE OLD PARADIGM

The Old Paradigm is essentially patriarchal. What we are calling the Old Paradigm, in which the institution of marriage is born is essentially man's struggle to survive as an isolated entity in an environment of separation, scarcity and strife. This survivalist paradigm is ancient programming rooted in the hind-brain: the often desperate struggles of the natural world. Hence, there is an in-born sense of competition in the Old Paradigm, man against man, family against family to 'make it' so that his family can get the things they need to have a better life, or just to survive.

As such in the Old Paradigm, marriage has been a respected, economically viable, social institution that has been charged with creating a loving partnership between individuals, and a safe, loving haven for children to be born into. But half of all marriages end in divorce (USA) and many still bear the scars from the structure they were brought up in, even as they try to do better for their own children.

The divorce rates and the social and economic strife we are witnessing are a reflection of a mind-structure - the Old Paradigm - falling down, and all its institutions with it as a necessary step in the evolution of consciousness on this planet. As tribes have shrunk to the size of the nuclear family (and even these are often overtly or covertly at war), and community largely abandoned, this model has become increasingly isolating. And where Love has flourished it is in spite of, not because of this old survivalist paradigm of isolation, lack, fear, worry and doubt.

For as we look around at the World that has been birthed from competition and patriarchy we see widespread destruction: war, holocaust, famine, water-shortages, social and economic inequality, disease, global-warming, pollution, mass-extinction, global debt, economic melt-down, stress, and suicide. For man has done whatever it takes to uphold 'me and mine' failing to realize that he has been taking from the very Earth that sustains him.

THE NEW PARADIGM

But the New Paradigm is upon us and within us. Together we slough off the dualistic, fear, worry, doubt and not-enoughness model and strive to abide in the abundance of the Universal Mind.

For in the Universal Mind, there is no lack, no problems, only unlimited solutions, and abundance.

What a thrill to be in form at this time with the challenge we've been given of problem-solving with our expanding awareness in order to flow much-needed solutions from the Universal Mind into the World. Each of us honored fully to bring forth our gifts, talents and skills fostered from the vantage point of the unique experiences and perspective we've been given. For we are all now uniting in a common goal that affects us all, realizing as we do that man is not separate from his environment; we are charged with birthing a new paradigm that places man as custodian of the planet and the Life that She nurtures rather than as an errant king with the power to take whatever is there.

RELATIONSHIP IN THE NEW PARADIGM

Within this new paradigm enlightened relationships flourish. Marriage is transmuted from coming together in struggle against scarcity into coming together to transcend negativity, to perfect ourselves from the inside-out so that we are the best possible versions of ourselves. And in this relationship, space opens up for us to bring our deepest gifts as a benefit to the Whole, to the planet and all of Creation.

2. EMERGING FROM MILLENNIA OF PATRIARCHY

Millennia of patriarchy leaves deep impressions on both the experience of being a woman and the experience of being a man and both sets of conditioning get brought into play in a relationship. It helps us to become aware of the kind of relationship that gets fostered in the old paradigm so that we can witness that patterning and conditioning within ourselves and our own relationships, in order to transcend it.

HOW PATRIARCHY CAME ABOUT

The qualities that rule in the patriarchal dynamic are the perverted or shadow forms of the Divine Masculine, the Divine Masculine being 'skillful action'. In the Old Paradigm of scarcity, lack, and competition, skillful action becomes brute force or manipulation for gain.

In this environment Woman[2], feeling herself vulnerable gives up true power - the power to transform pain into Love through Compassion (Divine Feminine) - and takes up the 'shadow' version of this: seduction.

WHAT BECOMES OF WOMAN IN PATRIARCHY?

For when violence and domination instead of Love rules, Woman must get close to the source of perceived power, a 'powerful' man capable of defending her and her children. Woman then gets reduced or reduces herself to one who must seduce power from a man through wielding the sexual power available to her. (Hence the obsession in the culture with clothing, make-up, and being seen as 'sexy' etc.)

In what we will call a sexually un-liberated culture such as the Old Paradigm, sexual power equates to the

---

[2] We use the singular 'Woman' instead of women and singular 'Man' instead of men deliberately because we are talking about woman and man as archetypes throughout the ages.

power that can be wielded over Man sexually through generalized cultural objectification of Woman. This dynamic pre-dates the monetary system but when that comes into play the dynamic is less about seducing the brute-force power of a man and more about getting close to financial power, hence the importance historically of finding a good provider.

The other option available to Woman in Patriarchy (for getting power) having given up the sacred power of the Divine Feminine, is competing for survival with Man in a Man's World. To do this she becomes a sort of second-class male, aping Man as a survival strategy, adopting the afore-mentioned corrupted form of the Divine Masculine: manipulation, calculation, and cunning or even a version of the brute force/macho side of the corrupted masculine, which is ubiquitous for heroines in modern movies. In this version of patriarchy, we also begin to see the sexual objectification of Man to a degree. So increased 'equality' between genders has not entailed a resurrection of the Divine Feminine but some shifts in the patriarchal model.

What happens to Woman in the Old Paradigm when her physical avatar is not or no longer considered sexually attractive? She feels dis-empowered, suffers low self-esteem and insecurities mount against the shallow values of the culture. She may turn to augmenting her form with surgeries of all sorts.

WHAT BECOMES OF MAN IN PATRIARCHY?

Man becomes stressed and, therefore, inhibited from reaching into his divine nature by the relentless pressure of being in control, being a ruler and a provider. Thus robbed of his eternal self the vibration of anger becomes the default make-up of his pain-body[3]. On top of that he is expected to at least have some capacity to defend and be brave, usually without any proper training! Thus, in a post-warrior culture man cultivates the skills of manipulation, calculation and cunning in order to survive in the rigors of competing in the financial model.

What happens to Man in the Old Paradigm when he is not or no longer set-up to make money? He suffers low self-esteem and feels inadequate, redundant.

---

[3] A body of emotional pain with a strong charge, a part of the false self.

ATTRACTION

Because of the overbearing values of the Old Paradigm, based on survival and ego, there is less chance of people coming together in attraction through a connection of Heart and Soul, Spiritual Energetics and shared higher purpose; less chance for the Heart to guide rather than the survival mind. As we move into the New Paradigm a new dimension of attraction opens up.

We the authors were fortunate to meet in a state of freedom, far beyond the reach of the worlds we had been brought up in.

I Maha had been traveling India for four months practicing meditation and had just spent six weeks on the Andaman Islands living in a beach hut, some of that time completely alone as a cyclone raged. And then making my way to an *ashram* in the southerly tip of India.

I David had just spent four months living at said *ashram* practicing meditation and undergoing a six-week Ayurvedic body purification program known as *pancha karma*.

Held in the high vibration of the *ashram*, far away from the patterning of the Old Paradigm with its conditions, judgments, criticisms and values and far away from the opinions of family and friends we were attracted by the resonance of our spiritual energetics, feeling a vibratory match that was recognizable and an instant joy. In this pure and ecstatic environment (it was the *ashram* of Mata Amritanandamayi Devi which translates as Mother of Immortal Bliss) where each was focused on shedding ego and communing with the Eternal Presence it was weeks before we would realize that what we had found together was a relationship beyond friendship for neither was looking for that and hardly recognized it as such. Why? Because there was no pain, no subtle feelings of vulnerability, insecurity, fear of rejection or attachment (feelings and notions we had both at one time or another unconsciously associated with love.)

...And it hit me, Maha, like as an epiphany in a feeling-tone, not an idea: *this is Love!*[4] And when we said

---

[4] I recognized the feeling (though it was on a different scale) from my first Awakening experience when coming into the same vicinity as Amma for the first time my Heart had leapt into spacious communion with the Eternal Presence, hearing the mantra 'Mother, Mother, Mother' inside myself.

goodbye after spending six weeks together in this Love, we would return to our respective lands still connected to the same Love within, without even having the conversation about when or if we would ever meet again, which was a paradigm shift for us both.

RESPECT FOR CHILD

Due to inherent biology, Woman bears the children. What the Old Paradigm cannot do is acknowledge the high role assigned (largely but of course not exclusively) to Woman of 'raising' them. This is because if a man or woman does not know their own true nature then the true nature of the children is also unknown. Therefore, the high role of 'raising' them is not seen as such; indeed the role of 'staying home' as it were, to raise the children exclusively is generally given little social esteem.

However in the New Paradigm there is not the strong delineation between the World of the children and the so-called adult world; they meet in the high vibration of the Mystery and this means there is not the same sense of giving up one's work but extending, sharing and deepening it. All are following their highest calling and so work comes to reflect this.

The work itself, whatever its nature, becomes less of a struggle as more understanding of the subtle levels of reality are uncovered, understood and accounted for; in short we inhabit a more compassionate, truly intelligent civilization that nurtures the totality of our being-ness.

Children of Zeus and of the Stars

The Old Paradigm sees children as empty vessels to be filled up with the information that will help them to compete, survive and achieve.

The New Paradigm, however, acknowledges babies are 'Children of Zeus, and of the Stars' and come through Whole and Holy with unlimited potential, innate healing power and unique gifts to discover and share.

The role of parents becomes to hold the space of Presence around these pure emanations so they may come into their fullest potential, inhabiting the totality of themselves and valuing who/what they truly are; what higher work than this?

RELATIONSHIP DYNAMIC OF THE OLD PARADIGM

Of course, it is not only cultural conditioning we inherit but also the power dynamic peculiar to our parents in our family of origin.

Hardly need we expand on the dynamic of a marital-type relationship in the Old Paradigm. Indeed, we are not interested in picking apart the Old Paradigm for the sake of it; for have we not all been birthed into it?

Temporarily, it lives within us, created out of us and provides us with the fuel to rocket into the New Paradigm. Only, we want to understand where the Old Paradigm ends and the new one begins.

The Old Paradigm, because it is based on the misstep that we are all isolated entities separate from 'God and his creation', is rife with power struggles and subtle curtailments of personal freedom.

Inadequate knowledge of what we are and how we are built leads to emotional warfare (bickering, bitterness, dissatisfaction, blame, jealousy, frustration, anger, hatred, impatience, inequality) as unconscious patterns based on family-of-origin dynamics are played out with little knowledge of how to process emotions because of over-identification with them.

Amid the confusion of who and what we really are, and the absorption in the fleeting world and its effects; disconnected from the Eternal Presence there is furthermore a tendency to try to hold on to our partner (in form) as though they were our very salvation. Thus, there is the tendency for Humans to attach and invest emotionally to form with everything they have. Indeed, there is the tendency to want to *own* one another in an earnest bid to have and hold close, something that is real.

And who can blame this yearning? For worldly love is derived from the supreme Eternal Love of our own true nature, that of God, but it is strongly filtered through layers of painful identity (our pain-bodies) attenuated and tainted by conditions and ignorance of an Absolute Truth. It is also abstracted from a blissful experience into an idea by the conditioned mind which cannot directly access it. So in the Old Paradigm there is a grasping and a clinging to the closest thing to 'the real thing'.

These types of relationships can with a degree of reciprocity be fulfilling (to the ego) and not fulfilling (to the ego and one's Spirit). In truth, many relationships are somewhere between the Old Paradigm and the New as we transition as a collective into higher understanding. But still not fulfilling in the ultimate way we need them to be if we are to transcend the Old Paradigm completely and harness relationship for the attainment of Self-Realization and the awakening of humankind. And not for those on the Esoteric Path of Marriage!

3. AGREEMENTS OF THE ESOTERIC PATH OF MARRIAGE

Enter the New Paradigm! A quantum leap from being ruled by and identified with form and mind into realizing the limitlessness of your true nature as consciousness. Plant your feet on the ground and gaze up at the sky! Feel it in your Heart! You are one with that spaciousness, that field of consciousness that is eternal and indestructible, that has an indefatigable love to create and play! Hiding behind the infinite diversity of its expression; playing 'hide and seek' and 'dress-up' with the many, as the many, is the formless, nameless, silent, Eternal Presence of the one consciousness.

"There is no idea of scarcity in this vast Presence that created every-thing out of no-thing! There is no lack, no limitation and no problems in this great universal mind. There is no worry, no fear, and no doubt."
– Dr Michael Bernard Beckwith

As we continue on our path of Awakening, we are slowly but surely becoming more and more identified with this spacious, loving, Being-ness out of which our very forms miraculously materialized inside a womb!

Something out of no-thing.[5]

The kind of marriage that the New Paradigm fosters is also a quantum leap from the old. Here we can stop the ancient wheels of karma turning, and birth a new paradigm within us where the Divine Feminine and the Divine Masculine are serving one another within us

---

[5] "I dare you," said Dr Michael Bernard Beckwith in an almost conspiratorial whisper, from a high state of ecstasy at the peak of one of his sermons at Agape one Sunday. "I dare you to create *something* out of *no-thing!*"

(regardless of physical gender) and in our relationship. As the polarities are balanced and harmonized, a creative power-house is born that can serve the planet in a mighty way. Any children raised in this kind of union will be a blessing to the World for many generations to come.

To enter relationship in the New Paradigm, to walk the Esoteric Path of Marriage, it is essential to make new agreements with yourself and with your partner lest you find yourself tacitly conforming to the agreements of the Old Paradigm without even realizing it.

<u>Agreement #1</u>

Commit Your Relationship To The Fires Of Self-Knowledge

Commit yourself 100% to Spiritual Liberation! Make an agreement with your partner to support each other 100%.

It is important to agree what your relationship is about, what it is for, for only then can you harness its astounding potential as a vehicle for transformation.

If both are strongly pulled towards Spiritual

Enlightenment and strongly pulled to be together, then a powerful agreement can be reached, to commit your relationship to the fires of self-knowledge.

This agreement entails that you solemnly agree not to build your partner's conditioned self or ego and your partner is solemnly agreeing not to build yours. For indeed, your partnership is now for something greater.

Agreement #2

Your Partner Is Not Responsible For Your Happiness

Contrary to the conditioning you will have received in the Old Paradigm where we come together in marriage in order to make one another happy and separate when we find we cannot, in the New Paradigm we ourselves are solely responsible for our own happiness.

This is important to contemplate for the false belief, that your partner is responsible for your happiness may be deeply ingrained in your unconscious mind. Notice how, when something 'goes wrong' or there is a feeling of unhappiness or you are not at Peace, there is a force within you, perhaps subtle, perhaps not so subtle, apportioning blame towards your partner. In some way, *you* are unhappy and *they* are to blame, so the story goes. In truth, the only source of true happiness comes from within you.

It really takes a big burden off of the relationship when we enshrine our Self as Sovereign of our own 'reality', seeing every experience as coming from the Universal Mind, from the Great Teacher within us, without exception.

Now we can look with interest at the turn of events; what is being shown to me? What am I being taught? How is my egoic structure being broken down through this? What is unconscious in me that is seeking to make itself conscious through this? In this way blame is replaced by Compassion, expanded awareness and Wisdom.

<u>Agreement #3</u>

You Are Not Responsible For Your Partner's Happiness

Your responsibility is to serve the Light of your own Self and play Mother to its innocent requests for Freedom, Peace, Happiness and Joy. Never play the martyr by ignoring the Truth of your own Heart. Never believe that you are responsible for your partner's happiness.

Do not stay in a relationship that does not serve your Happiness thinking you are doing the right thing. For ultimately there is only one Light to serve and if you are not serving it you are serving the shadow and more than just 'you' will be affected by its gloom.

Those who learn to honor the Light within themselves will not only be serving the Light in the relationship and in each other but also the Light of the World.

Give yourself to nothing that You are not.

Agreement #4

Die To One Another Everyday

Foster the habit of resolving your own pain within yourself and within the marriage hence try not to spread it out to family and friends who may hold onto the pain-body stories you share even long after you and your partner have moved on.

Through processing pain within your own selves *as it arises* the 'marital pain-body'[6] is dismantled before it gets a chance to draw breath. This means that at the end of each day any pain that we have created between us has already died and through intentional agreement, forgotten.

Dying to one another every day is more than just an agreement not to store away grievances for fuel in future furors, although this may be part of it. It is sacrificing your pain selves and each day being New, by which we mean light, unburdened and free to love.

That being said if pain from the past is present in your today, don't run away from it; give yourself the space to process the emotional charge in the now. You may still have to talk to your partner after the charge is neutralized, but you can do so with calm from a place of Wisdom.

---

[6] An account of the 'marital pain-body' is given in Chapter 5: Slaying the Dragon

Agreement #5

Let Your Love Be Unconditional (That Means Dropping All Agendas)

What is Unconditional Love? It is an effortless state in which all fear, doubt, and worry is transmuted and alchemized. It is empowerment of Spirit, expanded consciousness and the Wisdom of fully-felt experience. It knows It has nothing to be afraid of for it lives in the realization that there is no-thing more powerful than It. It is a being-ness connected to one's source, which projects no untruths onto others but naturally brings each moment into Its own loving embrace. It is Love beyond the need for mental understanding.

Marriage in the Old Paradigm is rife with unspoken conditions and agendas. Unconditional Love is reserved for mothers for their children and even so conditions - subtle and not-so-subtle – can and do creep in as the child becomes an adult. For example, sometimes a mother might pour so much identification into her child that she wants the child to fulfill her own un-lived dreams, perhaps forgetting that the child has his own unique path to create for himself.

In the New Paradigm the perfect Unconditional Love that a mother can have for a child becomes even possible for ones partner. How do we develop this kind of perfect love for our partner? It begins with finding Unconditional Love for ourselves, which is a progressive process. It begins to dawn naturally as our own inborn nature, as we learn to surrender to Life as our teacher and process our emotions.

Be vigilant and notice when conditions to your Love have crept in. There is no need to hunt them out, however, for impurities and conditions have a habit of rising to the surface for illumination. It may be agreements that are so fundamental in the Old Paradigm (e.g. those around status, money, etc.) that we have taken them for granted. Keep it pure.

Agreement #6

Your Partner Is Not An Object Frozen In Time And Space And Neither Are You!

In an old paradigm relationship, there is the tendency to enjoy building the 'idea' of one's beloved. This means building your partner's identity by identifying them as the sum of their likes and dislikes, judgments and opinions.

Indeed loving someone in the Old Paradigm seems to *entail* helping to pin someone down, and condense them into a strong sense of self with a 'unique' collection of opinions, likes, and dislikes.

In the process of spiritual awakening, we begin identified with form and name and gravitate from believing we are an object frozen in time and space to the realization that we are a process; formless, eternal, expanding and evolving through matter.

So, in this new agreement we cease to build or feed our partner's limited sense of self or project our own limited sense of self onto our partner. We give ourselves permission to live in and be the Mystery. We don't re-inforce fleeting likes, dislikes and states of mind, we don't confuse them with what our partner really is, pure potential, Eternal, Beauty-Love-Intelligence.

This also entails not 'holding' your partner to opinions and judgments, which can hold one back from the flow of Life itself. Allow yourself and your partner to be alive in the moment, fresh, original and new. Remember, as soon as we think of our partner solely as a thing e.g. an actor, a mom, a husband we instantly limit and confine them, narrowing their infinite potential into a comparatively myopic entity or role.

In truth, we are all of these things and none of them. At the very least give yourself and your partner, the freedom to change your mind based on the living information of the present moment. This opens up space for new creative expression and fresh experience.

The New Paradigm celebrates each individual as a unique emanation of consciousness. Because consciousness is infinite, it expresses itself differently through every single form in creation. There are no two snowflakes exactly alike, there are no two elephants exactly alike and there are no two Human Beings exactly alike. The entire Cosmos is the infinite expression of the Eternal One Life.

So your partner is indeed a unique and ever-changing emanation of consciousness but not by virtue of, nor confined to, likes, dislikes, opinions, and judgments.

Agreement #7

Be Aware of Promises

Promises both honored and broken are a source of suffering in the Old Paradigm. The reason for this is that, in truth, most promises are made from a limited part of ourselves, which doesn't have full access to all the information in the Kosmos with all of its many levels of reality; so it is not hard to see how promises made on the physical dimension can easily be usurped or give the promise-maker a hard time trying to fulfill on the promise. In short, (most often) a promise is given from one who does not have the supreme authority to make that promise, one who is taking responsibility for too much. (The ego).

On the Esoteric Path of Marriage become very aware of promises. Do not idly acquiesce to one who tries to illicit a promise out of you. A promise made in the past can forbid you to follow your feelings in the present, therefore forcing you to either go against yourself to keep the promise or break it and become a 'liar'. So try to pick your words carefully lest you wind up tied up in knots. Yes, strive to 'be impeccable with your word'[7] when it has been given (including when it has been given to yourself) but take into account the nature of reality and allow yourselves the necessarily wiggle room. What can be said instead of "I promise." is something like "Let us see how things unfold." By the same token, try to avoid the impulse to get your partner to "promise".

When you give others freedom, you liberate yourself.

Agreement # 8

Set A Good Example For Your Partner

Whether consciously or not we look to our partner as a guide, so better be a good one. It is said we become like those we spend most of our time with so you can honor your partner by honoring yourself; by leading by example you can empower the whole relationship.

No one likes anyone telling them what to do especially if it's unsolicited. If you feel by chance,

---

[7] The first agreement in Don Miguel Ruiz's landmark book *The Four Agreements*.

meditation would be good for your partner, lead by example and meditate more yourself and let your partner really witness your own transformation as you step into the fullness of your newly-empowered self.

If you are to become a teacher for your partner and ultimately, for the World, it starts with you. It must unfold effortlessly as one can only speak with authenticity or authority from ones *own direct* Wisdom-Experience and when listening-space is truly there. Only then can understanding be shared otherwise we are 'preaching to a rock wall' at best but more than likely creating more pain and separation - the exact opposite of what we wanted.

Agreement #9

Be The First To Lay Down Your Arms

In the Old Paradigm not 'backing down' is seen as a something like a virtue. But in the New Paradigm, being the first to lay down your arms is indeed heroic. Agreeing between you that you will both be the first to lay down your arms gives you a fighting chance of being able to move through painful conflict fast, transmuting old programs back into your own life-force.

The Esoteric Path of Marriage - or any path of Self-Realization or Spiritual Enlightenment - is not for the faint of heart. But show the way for your partner, and his/her ego may be humbled by your ability to climb down from a mental position and step into the unknown.

This is something that takes a lot of practice because it is going against the logic (survival-strategy) of the ego. If you walk away from an altercation with your partner, having lain down your arms but the voice in your head is still ranting and raving then you have likely fallen into the trap of acquiescing or you have gone against yourself in order to avoid conflict.

Having authentically lain down your arms there may still be an emotional charge in one or both of you but disarming yourself is the invitation for transformation; when properly executed, tears, Compassion, Love, and Unity may ensue.

Agreement #10

Your Partner Is Not Yours To Own

When a woman gives birth to a child there is the tendency - because the child comes through her - for her to think of the child as hers (or hers and her partner's) and on a certain level of reality this is, of course, true but in Truth, the baby is its own unique individual, a manifestation of pure potential, shot from Eternity.

Similarly, in the Old Paradigm in marriage-type relationships there is a tendency for one to believe that they own the other.

We are each gifted with access to Consciousness, what each of us decides to do with it, is each their own prerogative. In the New Paradigm relationship is a tool for your Liberation, not another thing to own, control or imprison you.

Agreement #11

Your Partner Is Holy...And So Are You

Your central relationship is with the One Consciousness, your deepest Self, that which manifests from the inside.

You are a unique emanation of the One Life and so is your partner.

In the New Paradigm, we can glimpse our partner beyond the veils of separation and as such it can provide the most sublime portal into the Eternal Presence of the Divine.

You can even acknowledge the holiness of your partner in gestures such as bowing to one another before making love.

Even reverence for inanimate objects helps to engender the Peace that comes to One who honors everything.

Tangentially, on the issue of artificial intelligence and robots, when deciding how much regard to give these creations, a great deal is made in science fiction of whether or not a robot is self-aware. The only important thing to realize is that *you* are conscious and how you interact with your environment has an impact on you, and you on it, as nothing is as separate as we think.

<u>Agreement #12</u>

Treat Your Partner With The Same Respect You Would Any Stranger

Over-familiarity is a one-way ticket to the Mundane. The Old Paradigm carries the vibration of the Mundane and we want to rise up out of this feeling-tone, never to return.

It may be tempting to have an 'easy going' dynamic where one is free to say anything and playfully tease one another, but this can easily wind up in nothing more than the average mundane relationship where in-authenticity, casual rudeness, and sarcasm are fostered. Instead, commit to treating one another with the same respect you would any stranger! This will help to keep it new and fresh in every moment and will create the garden in which sincere reverence and devotion for one another as gateways to the Cosmic Beloved/Eternal Presence can sprout.

Agreement #13

You Are Not A Safe-Haven For Your Partner's Ego

This is no idle pledge. For in the Old Paradigm, which is always tugging at us in the form of conditioning, thought-forms, and mental projections, a primary relationship such as a marriage is a place where one retreats to off-load and let off steam when the mental-emotional burden builds. However in the New Paradigm within the agreement we are describing it is not always going to be a useful practice.

What we are agreeing to is to not provide a safe-haven for our partner's false self or ego, ultimately built of pain. The important thing to realize is that though you may seem like the 'bad guy' when you hold space instead of joining in the feeding-frenzy, it is an expression of Selfless Love of the highest order, an act of heroism if carried out without judgment, because, rather than allying with your partner's false self - an act that will keep you both in shackles - you are inviting your partner to rejoin you in the Sanity of Presence, reversing ancient patterns of human suffering.

Practice makes perfect and it gets easier for ultimately when dealing with temporary entities like your partner's ego, remember…

Eternity has already won!

Agreement # 14

Be Guided By Your Own Light

In a partnership let there be no intercession between you and the Eternal Presence. If your partner has a strong connection to Spirit be sure to nurture your own direct line to God within yourself. There is no substitute for that direct relationship of connection to your own Source.

You transform yourself as you learn to Love your Self; you become the Unconditional Love Itself.

4. *PASHA** ON THE PATH OF PARTNERSHIP

*Pasha is a Sanskrit[8] word meaning "noose", "to ensnare" specifically, that which keeps us trapped in the Illusion (about yourself, the World, the nature of reality, etc.).

What follows in this chapter are some *pasha* to watch out for on the Esoteric Path of Marriage.

---

[8] The Esoteric Path of Marriage is for those from all spiritual and religious traditions and disciplines and for those who walk in the pathless land. Here and there, throughout the book we use Sanskrit words. Its origin is said by some to predate time and by others to have been revealed in the Hearts of meditators throughout the ages and indeed this has been born out by our own experience. Thus, Sanskrit is a language of the Heart, and belongs to us all; its high vibration is of the Heart and it is in that context that we use it freely herein to communicate the subtleties inherent in an esoteric path towards deeper union with Existence.

LOOKING THROUGH THE EYES OF OTHERS

The Esoteric Path of Marriage does not necessarily create a relationship that your aunts, uncles, momma, and cousins are going to look at and sigh, 'Ah what a perfect relationship'.

There may even be forces trying to pull you apart, as was the case when we, the authors got married. When a couple goes against the patterning and conditioning of a structure, those identified with the structural agreements may feel threatened and try to block the otherwise natural flow of evolution as the Old Paradigm dies to the New. Transcending these types of resistances is part of an evolution of consciousness that must be taken. Consider obstacles like these, on the path to Liberation, an invitation from God to trust the Wisdom of Love above all else. Hold onto your Hearts and take a leap of Faith.

Eventually, your relationship might be an example of perfection even from a vantage point from within the Old Paradigm, but it is most definitely not a relationship that is 'on show' as conjugal idyll. You have to let go of all of that and, holding space for the highest ideals, be impervious to all the opinions and prying eyes.

It is a relationship that may look from the outside, at times, ugly and even dis-functional because you are going to be rooting out one another's deepest pains, insecurities, weaknesses, false beliefs, vanities and selfish behaviors, all the stuff that isn't truly you. It is not about what it looks like from the outside!

Do not fall into the trap of judging your relationship through anyone else's eyes or values; that is a big source of suffering in old paradigm relationship and has torn many a marriage asunder.

SPEAKING ILL OF YOUR PARTNER

Never speak ill of your partner. If you need to vent, do so internally in your meditation by silently pouring out your Heart to the Eternal Presence within, asking for inspiration and guidance. If you still feel you need to talk to somebody, choose someone who is holding a high vibration of Truth such as a spiritual advisor or someone whose Wisdom and Compassion you trust. Don't confuse this with editing yourself by not speaking your *Truth* to your partner in the moment even if in the company of others. More on speaking one's Truth will be shared in Chapter 7.

KEEPING SCORE

Here we caution against doing things for one another *because* of something or in return for something: *I will do this for you because you have done that for me.* On the Esoteric Path of Marriage watch out for Old Paradigm conditioning around carrying out tasks or favors. Do not bargain with one another for it can lead to insincere action and you could run the risk of blocking the flow of enjoyment and Love. Do, or do not do. Love what you do and do what you love.

COMPARE AND DESPAIR

Resist the temptation to compare your journey or perceived level of spiritual advancement to your partner's (or anyone else's). For we are all wound up differently, having tied ourselves up with elaborate knots of survival and conditioning each with its own unique configuration, therefore our 'unwinding' will look different.

In Truth, we never know how close someone is to

Liberation and we never know how many battles someone has already fought and won.

MARTYRDOM

Martyrdom in marriage is going against oneself in order to serve another whilst upholding the role (to which one has become identified) of being self-sacrificing or saintly, which turns into unspoken resentment.

What is asked of one who has a tendency towards martyrdom is to reverse the conditioning and become what one is afraid of - being Self-ish - in order to follow the deepest calling of the Heart.

To really be of service to the World one has to be in tune with oneself and empowered in Spirit. When one truly serves their deepest Self, they are serving all of Nature.

It shouldn't feel *bad* in any part of you if you are serving your (highest) Self, which is the only One you should ever endeavor to serve. If you are flowing in the direction your Being is guiding you, it will feel unquestionably right. However, there are circumstances in which following your highest calling produces a painful conflict within you. You know it's 'right' at your core, but it hurts because a part of your false self is dying.

ATTACHMENT

You're in the jungle and you are swinging on the most perfect vine; you love this beautiful vine and the unique perspective it gives you. You've never experienced such a divine vine. Eventually, the time comes (maybe a life-time) when you have to let go of this perfect vine so that you can jump to the next.

You are in mid-air, afraid to jump, afraid to let go, you can't see beyond the vine you are in love with, so you would be leaping into the unknown, a leap of faith.

You cling and swing back and forth attached to your vine and eventually come to a halt, dangling in mid-air. You cannot progress from here. Eventually your arms will give way and you'll have to let go anyway but now you experience some kind of fall and will have to lift yourself back up again and start over. All of it and everything a learning and in time you will learn the art of non-attachment and be able to swing blissfully through the jungle embracing each and every unique vine with gratitude for the miracles of their existence and enjoying the ever-new perspective each one gives you. You might even be able to swing back through and visit vines you've adored along the way.

Those on the spiritual path may be concerned that having a marriage-type relationship with another will lead to attachment. It seems attachment is often misunderstood.

"Non-Attachment" can be an ideal behind which it is convenient for some to shelter when afraid to face their deepest stuff around relationship, gender, and sexuality. This can indeed, be complex work akin to opening Pandora's Box. Others may be afraid to love for fear of losing and getting hurt.

Perhaps non-attachment is not something to practice so much as it is something that naturally comes about through expanded awareness. Non-attachment does not mean that you don't love people anymore it means that due to your expanded understanding of who and what you are, your relationship is with Love itself. You abide in and serve the living moment rather than serving personalities or specific people. You respond to and are alive within the energetics in the present.

"Be like a tailor and always take new measurements."

-Mata Amritanandamayi Devi

In truth, non-attachment is a state of being in which there is absolutely no neediness.

I Maha, in processing some acute feelings of grief at the idea of there one day being "No more David" (in form) experienced a shift of consciousness entirely beyond attachment. It is a fullness, a state of awareness in which one feels Complete, Whole, Powerful, and Peaceful. It is a state that renders neediness for anybody absurd. It henceforth healed my fear of losing David, which had been a deep thorn in my Heart.

There is no way or need to strive for this state of consciousness through reason because it is entirely beyond the mind. However, if you have fear around losing your partner, it is possible to process it.

The important thing to realize is that if you have big 'work' with your partner then it will feel so good being around them, that for now, that is where you'll be. This is not an attachment to run from. This is a vibration to live in. Enjoy it and trust that as you inhabit your practices, your consciousness is ever-expanding in the direction of deeper and deeper levels of freedom and understanding.

That said, long periods of time apart may naturally open up (if it is necessary for your growth) for you so that you can explore the Light you hold independently of each other.

Allow yourself to love unapologetically and fully the expression of Life in every moment, (which is ever-changing), and all that flows through it, which is never-changing.

"I'm so renounced, I renounce renouncing."
                                    - Ramana Maharishi

<u>JEALOUSY</u>

Jealousy, whether it occurs within you or your partner needs Compassion rather than judgment. It is a painful, sticky emotion but can be released with Presence.

In the Old Paradigm, it is not uncommon for jealousy to arise even towards previous lovers - the vines that came before. Some expect their partner to deny the Love ever existed, failing to recognize Love as Eternal, the Love that came before or after being no exception. If jealousy arises in you, don't beat yourself up. It is merely unconscious pain coming up to be made conscious and it is through this process that we develop spiritually. Eventually, consciousness expands to include everyone and jealousy ceases to be possible.

The greatest gift of Love you can grant yourself and your partner is the freedom to love everyone with the same delicious intensity that you love each other. Sometimes a hug with a stranger can be a healing or even a micro love-affair as we commune in the space of the Heart. There need not be anything personal about it, and it doesn't have to be stored or held on to; allow the flow to continue. How healing it is to be open to the flow of Heart everywhere we go! Can we deny our beloved partner this Freedom?

This natural and delicious flow as described above is a paradigm shift away from the scenario of somebody with intention 'moving in' on your partner. In this situation, jealousy-pain may well arise within you. That is understandable but try to pay more attention to what is going on, on the inside of you rather than what you see through a filter of pain or what you *think* is going on, on the outside.

Having neutralized the emotional charge some (in Chapter 6 there is a full account of how to process emotions), you'll be in a more empowered place to discuss your concerns with your partner if you still have any.

Your partner and you enjoy a very special connection, a 'fit' that has a divine significance and purpose but the Love itself is no different from the Love you feel for all Beings. As Love, can we restrict our partner to loving only us and a few other family members and friends? Of course not! There is no hierarchy with Love and no ownership. Let yourselves be Free. Trust your Hearts to guide you.

The Esoteric Path of Marriage is not an invitation for an 'open' relationship but a relationship that is always open to the many forms of the formless, One Love.

INDULGING IN 'WOE-IS-US' MENTALITY

This is reinforcing co-dependent, self-destructive patterns, specifically, indulging a part of the 'marital pain-body' that vibrates at the frequency of victimhood - us-against-the-world - or even in some cases a partnership persecution complex.

Perceived set-backs are in a way, relished, by the 'marital pain-body' as they provide more fuel for the victim-story rather than embraced as opportunities to grow. This mode can assist the couple in remaining in limiting situations, locked together in comfortable yet ultimately dis-empowering programming at the expense of moving into something like Joy. 'The path' then becomes a test of one's ability to endure suffering rather than about discovering avenues of transcending it.

We transcend suffering through developing the ability to reside in our Selves to such a degree that the ebb and flow of Life's happenings both 'good' and 'bad' are seen as a divine play of consciousness that we become experts at embracing rather than resisting with stories of persecution.

PUSHING A RELUCTANT PARTNER

What if you experience a shift in perspective, but your partner has not, and is resistant, or perhaps not ready for the kind of intense commitment to Self-Realization that you yourself feel ready for?

Tread lightly friend, concentrate on your spiritual practices and avoid dogma. There is no faster way to push a reluctant loved one away from spiritual growth than to push the medicine on them, even if they sorely need it. Instead, be the medicine!

When your partner begins to experience more Patience from you, or a moment of unexpected Compassion, then it could be that the Gratitude he or she will experience will bring them into their Heart and into Spirit.

That being said if you have a partner (or anyone in your life) that tries to prevent you from your practices then that is a different story. That is abuse and oppression and that dynamic will need to be redressed for the relationship to be healthy.

If you are evolving beyond your relationship and you are receiving 'the Call' to Spirit that cannot be ignored, a call that your partner isn't receiving, then a choice lies before you. Are you empowered in Spirit, to be yourself? Or are you a life-line for someone else's false self or ego? Is your relationship nourishing your Heart and Soul?

In truth we get the partner we deserve; it is up to us how much authority we are prepared to give to the Heart and our choice of partner will be a reflection of this. The most important thing in any relationship is that everyone is empowered in Spirit to be fully themselves!

5. THE FALSE SELF AND THE PLAY OF CREATION

In order to ready ourselves for what lies ahead on the Esoteric Path of Marriage (teaming up with our partner to 'Slay the Dragon' in Chapter 6) let us first understand the nature of the Dragon and how it came into being.

THE ORIGINS OF EGO

How did we end up with ego? Why is there so much pain in the World? If the mind is the source of so much negativity then why do we have one?

What we can call the 'false self', 'surface-mind' or 'the continuous voice-in-the-head' (the ego) is a piece of programming, which evolved as a defense of the vulnerable Human who without claws, sharp teeth or wings was faced with surviving amongst the forests and jungles of the ancient world. It helped him to assess risk, calculate distances, and food and water availability, and warn him of genuine threats in the vicinity; providing cautionary thoughts about dangers.

As man's environment has evolved over the millennia, as the jungles and forests have been burnt, leveled and paved over, the quest for survival and the threats (and 'enemies') have radically altered. For it is no longer the contents of the jungles and forests Man must fear but Man himself.

For this survivalist program has adapted and developed a sense of self that is inextricably bound to the physical being that it is programmed to protect, that it has been given authority to defend. And this program is nothing if it cannot justify its usefulness for the purposes of survival. Thus, it can only survive if there is something on the outside to be afraid of (an enemy) and so in the comparatively un-hazardous habitat it has created for itself it must perpetually invent enemies and threats, now most often of a psychological and hypothetical nature. Of course the more power we give it, the more it manifests as a physical 'reality".

This piece of programming is built of consciousness. It is a creation that needs consciousness to identify with it in order to continue to exist. (Not merely to be aware of it but to be identified with/as it.) Therefore, its enemy is Unity. Its enemy is Peace. Its enemy is Presence and it will stop at nothing to avoid being in the present moment which it fears most of all. It lives in the future and the past. The more powerful it becomes, so improves its chance of survival as it wants what You already have whether you are aware of it or not and that is; Eternity.

So it continually pulls consciousness, from the Being and if necessary will even invent scenarios where it can be useful and gain leverage. This pulling of consciousness will keep going until a critical mass is reached wherein the whole World is governed by its focus on survival, competition, gain, superiority, and dominance. A paradigm in which such vibrations as Joy, Peace, Contentment, Benevolence and Unity are not truly valued. If given reign this program can take over a person to such a degree that the Being itself no longer feels it even has value. Indeed, this creation has no use for its creator, a source it instinctively knows is a threat to its survival. (In its ignorance it sees itself as the highest intelligence.) It is not the King but will gleefully be our Master if we believe its lies and misconceptions about us and the World.

And so we get the situation with the Human and this piece of primitive programming, where the tail is wagging the dog rather than the dog wagging the tail.

At this point, the human is compelled to reclaim its consciousness, hence reprogram this creation that has run amuck. For the program has morphed of late into a kind of 'Worm-tongue' advisor, feeling itself to be the King and now its main contributions to the Human Being are:

Worry

The source of mankind's suffering untold for eons. The source of furrowed brows, sleepless nights, mental illness and a whole host of physical ill-health. Some actually worry themselves to death. But most just live with a background feeling of unease (the person will hardly be conscious of, it is so 'normal') with intermittent hope; a flip-flop mind that waxes and wanes according to 'Worm-tongue's' counsel and its interpretation of the turn of events.

Self-Doubt

Its simple string of coding is such that this program has access only to a sliver of reality. As such it yields a myopic perspective and is convinced that its logic is all there is.

This belligerent advisor is unaware of the complex information the Human Being has access to on the level of Presence. If one identifies with this program instead of mining the rich information available, one is led to doubt ones divine guidance, doubt intuition, and doubt the Faith in one's Self.

Fear

Since the program's existence is very fragile it projects this fragility onto its host believing that it is made up only of mind and form, which could, of course, expire at any moment.

Thus has it designated itself with an impossible task,

to preserve that which is finite. Hence, it supplies the Human with an onslaught of self-preserving ideas, worst case scenarios, warnings of attack from perceived threats to itself and defensive counsel.

Lack

Since the Being it protects has deferred its sovereignty from its true seat of consciousness to 'it', (the ego, an isolated entity) the program is disconnected from the Source of Power and inter-connectedness and so it runs on a constant cycle of wanting. It has no grasp of the abundance of the Universal Mind and, therefore, its primary structure is: *Something's wrong, not enough!*

Self-Preservation

In its quest for survival, the ego, fails to take into account the feelings or life-value of other Beings or species it feels no affinity with. It produces thoughts from a vibration of separation and preservation for itself and what upholds it.

And it is worth noting that whilst the surface mind

makes its contribution (calculation, assessing risk, advising caution) it is the True Self, the quantum intelligence of the Being's consciousness that is connected to everything that truly guides man through dangerous situations. The following story illustrates this truth.

I Maha was in great peril on a remote tropical island of the Andamans. We had walked down a path through the jungle to a beach and as the day wore on, the group of travelers I was with made the foolhardy decision that instead of going back through the jungle we would make our way along the coast since someone had heard that the beach runs all the way along and takes you back to the main tourist beach.

The coast we were walking turned out to be hostile, with razor sharp rocks beneath the feet and huge fallen trees lying in our path since it had been ravaged by the Tsunami. The light was fading and the tide was coming in fast. The group fanned out, would we make it back along the coast before the light went or the tide entirely enveloped us?

Dressed only in a bikini (I had to take off my long sundress so that I could hike), some flip-flops and a rucksack I was the last one, lagging behind the rest at the back. It was every man for himself. One slip and I would have torn my skin to ribbons on the sharp rock now wet and partially submerged by the incoming tide.

The tide came into such a degree that I was sandwiched between the jungle on one side and the tide, now rushing around my legs on the other as I climbed over the fallen trees and jagged rocks in the gathering gloom. Yes, my faculties of reason were serving me well, duly noting the gravity of the situation but I recall that the surface-mind was busy pedaling its victim-story: "*I can't believe Christian has left me here at the back and hasn't even offered to carry my bag. Some of his stuff is in this bag. He's really showing his true colors in this situation.*"

But through no will of my own, my mind at some point stopped and I had entered a profound state of Presence, a high awareness, even feeling the aliveness of the rocks, feeling connected to everything as I moved on all fours as rapidly as the conditions would allow in this state of mortal danger. At one point, a large black reptile surprised me from the jungle. I kept moving from a state of Presence, utterly wedded to the micro-moment: the 'King' had taken back the control. Two hours or so of this intense focus in the midst of such great danger and I arrived at the beach in the pitch-black without so much as a scratch on my body. It pushed 'little me' beyond its limits and I was the awed witness and participant of the miraculous nature of Consciousness, the true intelligence connecting all.

THE BUILDING OF THE FALSE SELF

The false self's programming as discussed can be seen as the software of the Old Paradigm and fear, worry, doubt and lack are its modes. Like everything these modes carry a vibratory frequency and thus they are a dominant feeling-tone of the Old Paradigm into which we are born as babies.

We come in as babies not entirely helpless for we are powerful in Spirit; we have a strong ability to feel and freely express our Truth, a capacity that has been largely 'bred out' of the adults around us. What we don't yet have is a sophisticated way of translating these experiences through words but we can feel them and thus heal them and express them and protest them through crying.

Bit by bit - as our free expression is brought under

control, we give up this power. The adults around us convince us it is better to have their approval and love than this ability to wail out our emotional pain through deep-feeling. Understand we can be so subtly sensitive as little ones and so vulnerable to the opinions and feelings of our parents that it may only take one landmark incident as a baby in which our emotional expression was met with resentment or coldness to disconnect us from our inner power. We are not our parents, but we identify with their resistance and feel responsible for their pain.

Eventually, we believe the programming, which is running all around us that we are isolated forms without a source of Love/Power within. They also convince us (or we convince ourselves) to fear their disapproval, which we translate as little ones into the withdrawal of their love, which can be catastrophic to us now we have abandoned our Love/Power within.

Now when we begin to experience pain we are not at full liberty to feel it and so we develop protection and preservation strategies, defaulting to the software of the Old Paradigm.

What are we to do with this information as parents?

Simply to *acknowledge* that the baby is having a rich emotional and spiritual life even before the mind with its capacity for memory has been developed, is a paradigm shift. Understanding that our baby's tears, may be related to subtle feelings of emotional pain (that the adults around them may not even be aware of), we can come into Presence and help to support our little ones without the mental resistance that will confuse these sensitive Beings and make them at odds with their natural healing functioning.

A small child might be called a 'cry-baby' when he is only feeling and expressing his pain. Now he knows he is not permitted to cry, for by doing so he has caused distress and made himself a burden to those he loves, those who know better than him. Now he must learn to dam his feelings. When the emotional pain comes in, he puts up a wall of resistance, not wanting it to show itself on the outside and it is stored away as a layer of the pain-body. He becomes what he is not for the World because the World no longer feels safe for him to be who he is.

Thus slowly robbed of our true power we look around at the World, at our older brothers and sisters and at our parents, to see how *they* are getting *their* power. It may not be conscious but we look to see what's working for them, and as a survival strategy we clone their false selves on top of our Selves. In ways such as these are our false selves built.

So the pain-body is made up of layer upon layer of resistance and protection which began to be constructed the moment the child felt that it was necessary to help him to survive in his World. To reiterate, the 'pain-body' is part of our false self, the more highly charged pain that we have stored within us. Certain scenarios and circumstances will trigger this energetic body and strong emotions will be experienced. It is the part of us that is so angry and hurt that it has lost its power, a conscious connection to its True Self.

In a relationship, it is easy to see how conflict arises with these outmoded and redundant programs still functioning.

In the New Paradigm, we become the witness of this programming and endeavor to calm and purify the mind through awareness practices and the inner arts. Once the mind is calm, we can be the recipient of our true, divine thoughts: Inspiration, Enthusiasm, Genius, Epiphanies and Revelatory Insight. We then create from the deepest parts of ourselves without any unnecessary filters damming our flow.

In a partnership, there is double the chance of becoming identified with false self-programming but also double the opportunity to catch it if we work together.

PERSONALITY TRAITS OF THE FALSE SELF

Pain-bodies are complex and built of a variety of different vibratory patterns. But they all have some things in common; they are all 'designed' to 'protect' the Being; none of them have a life source of their own and so have their own special way of extracting it, by getting consciousness (you) to identify with it; and all are born of the Old Paradigm.

What is the configuration of my pain-body? What is its emotional flavor, its vibratory frequencies? What kind of situations, vibrations, ideas, and scenarios, trigger it? What kind of a pain-body does my partner have? This kind of reflection or investigation can be useful, because spotting the programs at work within you creates space between what is You and what is not. Approach the subject with the emotional aloofness of a scientist, with interest, not judgment.

Upon examination, you will likely notice that you *regularly* identify with *several* of the following to one degree or another. They are all gremlins and come with a warning: don't water and don't feed.

Have Compassion for the mind,
but don't give it an inch!

The Approval Junkie

Created in the kiln of punishment-reward parenting techniques the Approval Junkie has been unconsciously trained like a dog. Having approval has felt so good and disapproval so bad that the poor Approval Junkie, hardly knows who it is, still less, what it is. It makes decisions through the minds of others, decisions that will be met with tribal approval and one afflicted must struggle, agonizingly against its conditioning in order to walk in the light of spiritual Liberation.

The Joker

Living on the surface and afraid of depth the Joker seeks to let out the 'pressure' of every situation especially those that may get close to healing, feelings, and heart-connection by diffusing it with a well-timed joke to which all have been conditioned to laugh whether they find it funny or not. In this way does the Joker sustain itself and is guaranteed 'power' until the 'space' or silence the Joker is most afraid of - the space of the Heart - can be held. In extreme cases, the Joker is passive-aggressive and can only express its feelings through jest and so is ultimately dis-empowered and frustrated. It may even belittle the Joy of others, becoming a tyrant through its jest.

The Judge

The Judge wants to inhabit a fair world as judged by its own standards born from its myopic perspective and limited understanding. It is not aware of the intricate nature of the law of *karma*, that every action has an equal and opposite reaction - for though the Eternal Presence does not judge, it never forgets.

And so it assumes the role of the supreme arbiter of justice and often cannot help but vocalize its judgments, canvassing the opinions of others to garner support. But on the inside the Judge is not as robust as it may appear for it turns this same ascorbic judgment on its own self with exhausting, relentless regularity.

The Critic

Similar in vibration to the Judge, the Critic makes its living by making habitual comparisons between things, people, situations, and experiences that it comes across. There is a degree of holding on - to the past - for the Critic is not living wholly in the present, appreciating the newness of each moment but is (self)-condemned to compare the now with the past in a bid to find meaning and value. The Critic has not yet tapped into the miracle of the existence of the manifest world.

The Nay-sayer

It is its job to block the flow of divine inspiration. It just feels too scary to dream of something greater. What if those dreams didn't work out?

Time Monkey

Habituated by the clock, the Time Monkey is a slave to Time. It lives permanently in the near-to-mid future, never present with or able to enjoy the Peace of the present moment because its mind is rushing it on to the next, the next task, the next appointment, the next chapter, where its salvation will be.

It has given Time far too much reality and it has become a burden, which it forces onto others. Even if there is little Time Monkey in you, the tyrant that runs the Time Monkey will try to run you also if you let it. Keep your own tempo with the Time Monkey! And remember God never rushes anyone.

The Devil's Advocate

The advocate or representative of the Devil (the ego),

the Devil's Advocate, knows nothing of the Eternal Presence. It takes on the responsibility of and makes a virtue of speaking up for doubt which it sees as 'reason' in the face of a quantum reality it cannot access from its linear perspective.

The Interrogator

The interrogator may be kindly, playing therapist to those around by asking questions, assuming everyone likes to talk about themselves (projection) or may be more of a social predator, seeking to be in a power position, which may be rooted in social anxiety. Preferring to be the cat rather than the mouse the latter survives through almost aggressive questioning, deflecting the attention from its insecure self. If caught by this cat 'the mouse', bowing to social convention, must answer the Interrogator and often winds up saying more than he is comfortable saying or becoming defensive. He walks away feeling somehow reduced for the Interrogator has unconsciously put 'the mouse' in a box and walks away feeling subtly 'more' having been 'fed' by 'the mouse'.

The Tyrant

At its root, this patterning is an expression of resistance towards Life. Deep down the Tyrant feels small and insignificant and is driven by its own anxiety or unease to try to control its environment and those in it to the best of its ability.

The Know-All

The Know-All has invested its consciousness exclusively in the intellect. Indeed, its sense of identity has become inextricably bound up with the thinking mind and with being the one who knows. This is a lot to uphold! It often has a killer instinct and will bend the discussion in any way it has to in order to win, stopping at nothing. The Know-All may even summon up a few white lies or be liberal with the facts for its life depends on winning this verbal battle.

The Yes-Man

The Yes-Man is afraid of conflict and so goes to great lengths to agree with whatever it feels is the most prevalent/dominant force or opinion in the room often changing its allegiances at the drop of a hat. As such it is out of touch with its own feelings and opinions. It has become so accustomed to conflict-avoidance and agreeing that it is almost hard-wired NOT to speak its truth for it spends so long in social survival that its truth is buried.

The Victim

The Victim lives in an unjust Universe because the Victim has not yet surrendered to Experience as a teacher, to assimilate it into expanded understanding. The Victim, therefore, feels on some level as though Life is out to get them. It holds on to its past, painful or tragic experiences and lives in its story. There is a feeling of weakness and the Victim holds a defensive stance, carrying a self-pity vibration and often the vibration of blame towards others. These vibratory walls block one's ability to process Life's lessons and step into one's unique expression of Divinity.

The Monster

A more obvious version of the Tyrant, the Monster is usually birthed out of a trauma background. The Monster is built of anger, fear and, self-hatred to varying degrees. Usually a patterning that feeds through the pain of the man-woman relationship dynamic in the Old Paradigm. It is an attacking energy and is often unconsciously attracted to the Victim. Together they can continue to uphold one another.

It has felt the pressure of the struggle for so long (a struggle for which it feels responsible, for it 'should' be in control of but isn't) that it has never gotten to know its divine gifts. Feeling hated and reviled, loaded down with pain it cannot process, it attacks as an unconscious cry for help.

As we grow in wisdom and understanding, we trade these false selves in for Higher Truths.

CHARACTERISTICS OF THE TRUE SELF

Ego is built on a false belief of inferiority or superiority; the True Self resides in the Unity of itself and entertains neither. It is built out of the high vibrations or feeling-tones of Joy, Bliss, Peace, Enthusiasm, Unconditional Love, Devotion, and Rapture, and its modes are Humor, Patience, Levity, Sincerity, Ease, Grace, Freedom, Trust, Confidence, Compassion, Calmness, Discrimination, Ingenuity, Boldness, Clarity, Truth, Tenacity, etc.

6. SLAYING THE DRAGON

"The ultimate dragon is within you, it is your ego clamping you down."
                                                    - Joseph Campbell

THE ELEPHANT IN THE ROOM

The key to walking the Esoteric Path of Marriage is learning how to process your own emotions, allowing them to pass through so that you no longer identify yourself or your partner as the emotions. This does not mean pushing them away, as they have a value and hold a key to our Self-Realization.

If your partnership is new and you are a vibrational

match, it may take a while for certain functions of your relationship to manifest. In a conscious relationship where we are practicing daily going-inside we are mining layers of personality made out of identification with dis-empowered moments and un-felt pain. Consequently, we will find ourselves at some point butting up against one another's deeply-rooted patterning in a uniquely useful way.

Processing your emotions is all about becoming increasingly aware and in touch with how you feel. We are talking about entering deeply into a dimension of ourselves that we have spent much of our lives running away from.

As we enter Presence, calming the mind, we drive our attention inwards into ever more subtle sensation. We become inner-explorers. This type of meditation practice builds awareness and greater access to depth of consciousness within oneself. It is a progressive process of becoming a deeply-feeling being in every moment, not pushing away a single felt-sensation or emotional vibration from your energetic field but dissolving them in an embrace of consciousness that is ever-expanding. That is Empowerment; that is Enlightenment.

> *"We are made to be clearing-houses for experiences, not storage-houses."*
> - S. N. Goenka

As we know, the continuous thoughts from the surface-mind are often erroneous, defensive, attacking, judgmental, anxious and fearful, propagating that duality. This is because the surface-mind misinterprets events and situations without having access to the wider cosmic purpose of things.

Our feelings hold the key to the truth, however because they are direct information of the vibratory experience we are receiving in the moment, if we aren't resisting them in the moment. If we *are* resisting them, they get stored up, one on top of the other, layer upon layer. Now in each moment we are not only receiving the vibratory experience of that moment but also carrying the unwieldy stack of layers from other previously un-felt moments. And we go on this way, interacting with our partner through all of these layers. There's an elephant in the room! Isn't anyone going to acknowledge it?

This may go on largely unnoticed until we are

triggered, and what we experience is some emotion, for the layers of a certain frequency has reached a critical mass. There is an emotional outburst and from there our partner, will either be able to hold the space of Unconditional Love or will buckle under the weight of their own emotional layers, themselves tipped over into critical mass. This could develop into a marital battle with painful stories on both sides about whose fault the argument was, who started it, who shouldn't have said this or that. Old wounds are also given the chance to re-open to restate their grievances at this time. It's pain on top of pain.

MAKE SPACE TO FEEL

If we learn, through practice, to detect sensation in the body *as or before* it reaches critical mass, then we can stop whatever it is that we are doing and 'read' the information that the intelligence of our being-ness is sending us. Then we can step away and enter the dimension of feeling more fully by turning our consciousness inwards and giving Presence to that which wants to be felt.

We can hold up our hand, palm facing our partner

and say: "Wait, I need to process" or better still just begin to process. Set it up that way as an agreement that when you need to process on the inside you are no longer required to be there for your partner on the level of mind to answer questions or converse, for you are there for yourself, and thus automatically for them. For all is experienced as one in the dimension of Presence, and this is important nay heroic work!

Perhaps you can come to see all your feelings, all the sensation in your body and energy field as your own children, crying for your attention. After all, have you not, on some level of yourself, created each and every one of them? Thus we do not want to look the other way, ignore and pretend we do not know them.

DROP THE STORY

In the heat of conflict, your mind is peddling a story. It will be convincing, listen closely, it will be appealing to you to make a case for this situation, this moment to be an exception to the Law of Peace, that this is something you need to give away your Inner Peace for if you are to survive.

Notice the vibration of the words. Can you calm the vibration with your awareness? Of course you can! You're a Warrior for Peace. Do not believe the story. Drop the story of this painful vibration of duality. Even if you feel wronged by the Universe in ways you couldn't previously have imagined; drop the story! Enter the Presence, allow whatever is there to be alchemized and let it renew you. A fresh understanding will come.

TRANSCEND ORDINARY NEGATIVITY

Depending on the dynamic of a relationship there may be 'common or garden' negativity in the form of irritability, impatience or a clash of preferences. Depending on the nature of the relationship this will either be expressed or suppressed; verbalized or internalized. Either way it contributes to the 'marital pain-body'; it is the little things, the moment by moment interactions that maketh a marriage heaven or hell.

No-thing is worth the price of your Peace!

Nothing at all!

On the Esoteric Path of Marriage we set ourselves high ideals because we recognize there are no little pains; they all take us into the mundane vibration of the Old Paradigm. Make a commitment with each other not to create any new pain if you can help it. It gets easier with practice and there will continue to be fewer layers of 'otherness' to clash against, fewer layers blocking the flow of Life. The more Space you hold, the more you may be called upon by the Universe to hold that space, even little moments can have grand significance.

THE MARITAL PAIN-BODY

The marital pain-body contains the history of the couple from the perspective of the false selves; the dissatisfactions, the compromises, the struggles, the 'mistakes', the regrets, past battles, the tragedies, infidelities, betrayals, jealousies, sacrifices and seemingly small annoyances.

It is not aware there was ever any Love between you.

The marital pain-body, when activated can link up to the individual pain-bodies. It can loom so large that it eclipses all light that ever came before it. Thus identified with its story we believe, in those moments that our entire relationship has been a debacle, nothing more than a struggle, a misstep that has taken away our freedom, and maybe even our whole life a total failure, or whatever the story is.

Thus even if you have spent three days in actual bliss and the pain-body is activated it can convince the couple, like a collective hallucination, that the entire relationship has been nothing but misery and conflict.

IT'S JUST PAIN TALKING

If as your pain-bodies clash you find yourself saying 'terrible' things to one another, do not take it to heart or hold on to it. If your partner, in one such moment says something terrible to you, make some distance between your beloved and their pain by saying "That's just pain talking!". Or, after one such heated confrontation burns down to its embers you can say to one another: "That was just pain talking." Ahhh, how beautiful it is to know what you are, and what you are not, and release yourselves from holding on, and blame and building more identity out of pain.

TRANSMUTING A DIFFERENCE OF OPINION

For us, the authors, the clashes we have experienced have largely been as a result of the process we are in. We have mostly found ourselves wrangling amidst the challenges of helping one another to heal, drawing attention to one another's patterns, pressing against layers and exacerbating emotional wounds. When you and your partner are really deep in the process of Self Realization, you may arrive at layers of yourself that are jagged and raw. Those last bits of pain/identity will fight till the bitter end to defend themselves; the ego is fighting for its life! The following approach is with this kind of conflict in mind as opposed to a difference of opinion that may be calling your Hearts in two different directions.

So you and your partner find yourselves identified with opposing points of view. In the Old Paradigm, this means war because if either of you are going to give it up and be wrong then something is going to have to die right there and then. You might be able to feel a squirmy feeling inside when your opinion, which at times may even be arbitrary, is being challenged by your partner. Observe the rigidity in your body-mind, is there a pain that doesn't want to die?

In a noble act of self-sacrifice, you can lay down your arms, climb down from your mental position, realize you may have an opinion, but you're not going to let it define you and become humble, become seemingly less-than, just for a moment. For in an awakened relationship your partner will be so grateful for the sacrifice and will inwardly worship your humility, for now your partner can let their mental stance go also, stop pretending to be small and once again reconnect with his/her more expanded Self and the Love between you can be experienced once more.

If your partner is calling you on something and you find this one hard because you feel attacked and this is bringing up your defensive programming then try setting aside your emotional charge and *imagine*, for the sake of breaking the pattern, that your partner has a point, is not really attacking you and is only trying to help you. This imagining will give you a new focus, help you to lower your fists so to speak and give you permission to drop into, so as to dissolve, the pain that you have been so fiercely resisting. If your partner is Present, you may be able to meet in the land of feelings. Compassion may ensue, tears may fall and out of that sweet feeling new insights, beyond what either stance had been able to envision may arise.

"Whether you resist or you give it up willingly, your ego will be taken from you; because only then will you be happy."

-Mata Amritanandamayi Devi

HEALING ACUTE CONFLICT

What if your difference of opinion does not feel arbitrary? What if your conflict is rooted in pain that has a strong story, to which all or some of you is identified? What if it feels as though this one can't be quietly processed on your own or let go of? There are times when certain emotional vibrations reach a critical mass and a pain-body has been triggered. This may be happening on both sides of your relationship; a bitter row is brewing. There may be no way through other than to let your pain speak. When this is done consciously, when space is held for the pain to have its say, this can bring a powerful healing, like drawing poison from a wound.

Here's how it's done, we call it 'Cushion Talk'.

"Cushion Talk"

Set up two cushions on the floor. The one who is ready to speak, who perhaps has the most emotional charge sits on one of the cushions. The other one of you sits on a chair and holds the non-judging witness space as the one on the cushion is given permission to let their pain speak, to give the pained one inside them a voice. This voice is directed at the second cushion which represents the other.

Then you can swap over, taking it in turns to hold space and speak using the cushion as a bridge to non-personal communication. It is important not to hold back in any way when you are the one on the cushion and it is equally important that when you are the one on the chair that you do not judge but hold loving, compassionate space. That is, take nothing personal! When pain is met with Compassion rather than anger, a healing takes place that is both sublime and magical!

Do however many rounds of this that you need to do

until there is sufficient distance between you and your pain (you and your 'stuff') and you are able to consciously face one another and have a calm and fruitful discussion.

CONFLICT AVOIDANCE

If we live on the surface in a fixed egoic dynamic in which, for example, one person is passive the other dominant then we may be able to co-exist relatively peaceably by conflict-avoidance without too many big blow-outs. This is a survival strategy with no chance of spiritual growth if feeling is avoided. The pain-body will continue to build perhaps manifesting as mental and physical dis-ease.

HEALING ANGER

Having Compassion for anger might be one of the biggest spiritual challenges out especially when that anger is attacking you. Being deeply present in the felt-vibratory experience, we will eventually realize that anger is really just pain. It shouts and clenches its fists and curses but really it wants to sit down and weep if only it knew how.

Being identified with/as intense anger is very painful. The Being underneath wants to be free of its layers so badly so that it can feel the bliss of itself once more. Remember the faster and more thoroughly you can dis-identify yourself and/or your partner as anger, the easier it will be for you/them to dis-identify from it too.

You or your partner may be struggling with your own victimhood pain-body at the same time so it is an almost impossible challenge. Don't worry or blame yourself if you slip up. You will have chance after chance to heal this and each time, if you do the work of dis-identifying, it will get easier as a degree of 'this is not really me', opens up.

As you commit to your inner arts practices trust the pain is coming off, not on, you are becoming lighter and brighter even when you are in the eye of a storm.

MANAGING EXTREME PAIN-BODIES

From Monster to Magnificent: Transmuting Your Mr. Hyde.

Though living as a conscious Being you may still have visits from an extreme pain-body, the shift into which will be so dramatic it will feel energetically like a freight train slamming into you and will seem as though an imposter has taken you over as in the strange case of the dual personality of Dr Jekyl and Mr. Hyde.

This kind of pain-body is born out of a trauma background where a child has experienced sustained periods of oppression of Spirit, fear or neglect. It helps to know: that anger or rage isn't you. It can be transmuted no matter how long it may have been with you or when it was created.

In the energy of that pain, if we let it, it overwhelms us, in that moment it becomes us. But if we can hold onto our Presence we can transmute it. It becomes information, clarity, wisdom, understanding, and fuel for self-empowerment and evolution.

Perhaps you can detect some subtle feelings of pride mingled in with the anger that is fuelling the justification of a show of strength or power. But though it may seem that it is all powerful - and the Victim's fear can feed this reality - it is really weakness disguised as strength and has no life source of its own, outside of the reality we give it; it is parasitical. Anger always feels justified in the moment but perhaps it never is[9].

Helping Heal a Partner with a Case of Mr. Hyde

At first you may be terrified of Mr. Hyde, bewildered, and confused for the vibration is of anger and hatred and violence and could well be directed at you. You may have no idea what triggered it, it may seem to be nothing at all. Out of seemingly no where an eruption of a vile monster.

The more conscious the relationship, the less likely a pain-body will inflict physical abuse. But it may carry the vibration of violence and may even inflict violence on itself, throw stuff across the room or unleash a volley of insults. In these moments, you may wonder: where has my Beloved gone? And who is this imposter?

---

[9] There is such a thing as 'Divine Ire' but this comes from beyond the personality from Wisdom and Compassion and is a healing for the recipient (sometimes seen amid the Guru-Disciple relationship). But it is an anger with no shadow that feels like Love.

Confronted with a pain-body like Mr. Hyde, it may take a while for you to see your own. For these visits from Mr. Hyde will elicit emotions such as outrage, bewilderment and a feeling of being violated. With the intensity of what Mr. Hyde is throwing out, you may feel utterly identified with those emotions, utterly identified with playing Victim to the Monster. So rather than diffusing the situation, the victim pain-body may only fuel the monster which fuels the victim still more creating a vicious cycle of pain; the serpent devouring its own tail, ensnared in an endless drama of futility. Such is Man's lot if he doesn't hold up his hand and heroically declare 'No more, it ends here!'. Driving our consciousness inwards in these moments, we literally heal the 'sins' of our Fathers. You may be working through deep ancestral patterning on both sides, so have courage.

The key is realizing that your partner's pain exists within them whether you are there or not. So although you may have unwittingly scratched the wound, it's not really personal towards you, it was created long ago before you were even on the scene!

The second epiphany is, if Mr. Hyde visits, your partner is in tremendous pain. If we can sweep our own pain-body aside, that is identified with being wronged, (by spotting the Victim's thought-frequency and refusing to ally ourselves with it), we *gnow* that anger is, in fact, pain with a specific vibratory frequency and flavor. Then our natural Compassion will be activated. Only in this way can we once and for all free Mr. Hyde from this world.

Though it may be useful to understand what triggers our Beloved's pain, be aware it cannot be avoided; something is going to activate that stored pain (probably you). For, on the Esoteric Path of Marriage every single emotional wound - past, future and present - must come to a head, burst and heal, leaving no scar.

If either of you can get yourself to a place of being the witness, even to a small degree, you have won. With practice, the witness space will open up more and more within you, now you cannot fail, just keep being brave and doing the work.

In the Old Paradigm, these kinds of outbreaks are grounds for divorce. But on the Esoteric Path of Marriage where a relationship has been consciously steered towards Absolute Truth they are a crucible for transcending pain and deepening Compassion. This approach of developing Compassion for anger within a marriage represents a radical step forward for Human Civilization!

Of course, we are not advocating staying in an abusive relationship! An abusive relationship cannot exist on the Esoteric Path of Marriage, for we have vowed to use partnership as a vehicle for Truth.

DEVELOPING COMPASSION FOR YOUR SELF

From Victim to Guiding Light

Tears are not understood in the Old Paradigm. They are seen as a weakness by men and women. But the New Paradigm ushers in the strength and healing power of tears as a manifestation of Compassion. If we are to harness this strength and power, we must learn how to cry consciously.

When you begin to cry either out of a clash with your partner's pain-body or as a result of other earthly happenings, become very present inside yourself. Notice the torrid thoughts passing through your mind, the narrative your mind is giving you for 'why' you are crying. Tears become a holy sacrament when we dis-identify from the victim's story - this will take surprising strength - and drop deeper into feelings in the Heart.

It may sound like something small, but it is a paradigm shift to cry in the space of the Heart as opposed to from the mind-space of the victim. You will know if you are crying from the victim if the tears are accompanied with feeling sorry for yourself; such and such events shouldn't have happened, etc. You know if you're in Presence if in the crying there is also an unmistakable empowerment of Spirit.

Sobbing through the emotional charge whilst not identifying with the story is Power. You don't need anybody on the external to see your point of view or comfort you as from this place, you are receiving Compassion from the eternal Heart of Mother-Father God. On the absolute level you are inviting the Compassion of the Universe into your Self, you are becoming Compassion, and it is a beautiful thing. *Compassion* is from the Latin stem *compati* and means 'suffer together'. In these rich moments the Eternal Presence is 'suffering' with you: you are not alone.

Perhaps you will reach a stage of devotion where your tears are tears of ecstasy and bliss overflowing like a soft fountain from a Heart in communion with the Source of Life itself. A few moments of tearful communion with God is worth hours of seated meditation so count it as a blessing if you can allow your Heart to connect to the Presence in this way and know that as you expand in consciousness these tears are not just for you, you are transmuting the pains of the World.

EXPANDING YOUR AWARENESS INTO THE WORLD

Through the practices contained herein your pain-bodies will be slowly relieved of their power and alleviated of their skewed reality until eventually, with persistence, there will be more distance between you and your thoughts and the length of time your pain-bodies are 'at large' will become shorter and shorter, they will become wraith-like with hardly any power at all.

As you expand in awareness and the layers of separation between you and 'others' begins to dissolve you can (and must) become open to feeling the wider critical mass of humanity. As we develop into deeply feeling Beings in every moment, this becomes our service to God, to unburden the pain of others by developing a deeper and deeper willingness to accept, experience and feel sensation without judging.

Indeed eventually, we come to see it as our own regardless of whose 'stuff' it might on some dimension of reality seem to be. When we live deeply in the moment in this way, without resistance to what flows through us, we are liberated. What a delicious paradox this is!

7. COMMUNE-ICATION

LISTENING IS THE KEY

A relationship in the New Paradigm is the perfect arena in which to practice truthful communication and this will overflow into every single interaction you have as an awareness of the Eternal Presence behind all form begins to take hold as a lived experience.

Notice how well you listen to your partner. Give more preference to the feelings that arise within you when you are listening to your partner, than to the thoughts that arise that may be pulling you away from what your partner is trying to communicate. Listen to your partner with your Heart, in a state of as much Presence as you can master. Not just when the two of you have 'stuff' to talk about but whenever your partner talks to you. Let any thoughts that arise whilst your partner is speaking roll on by. Truly listening to your partner when they are speaking, is an act of love - and will be felt as such. It will help your partner to speak with more awareness and not 'run off at the mouth', willy-nilly. This will make for more fruitful conversations and deeper, more truthful commune-ication.

SPEAK YOUR TRUTH

Finding your Truth, is the first challenge of speaking your Truth because old paradigm conditioning often leaves us disconnected from something as simple as *gnowing* our own feelings. There may be filters in the way that are unconscious because they have been there so long and because it is 'normal' to have such filters up in the Old Paradigm, so they can go unnoticed. Fears of being judged or disapproved of, making someone angry or having love with-held from us all hold us back from being able to access our Truth. Is there any with-holding in your relationship, even subtly so?

On the Esoteric Path of Marriage, your relationship prepares the ground for all other relationships so it is important to learn to find your Truth and speak it in communications with your partner. Give yourselves permission to change your minds also. Even after the moment has past we may realize that we didn't speak from our deepest truth and there is still chance to rectify it. Eventually, we want to get to a place where we are always able to speak our truth effortlessly in the moment because if we are able to always speak our truth we are very close to being our true Selves. So speak your Truth even if, at times, your voice wobbles with emotion as can happen when one is learning to speak one's truth, opening up the throat and releasing repressed emotions. Even if by doing so, we send ripples of astonishment amid our audience. It takes practice and gets easier as egoic structures dissolve.

Through spiritual practice and learning to speak one's Truth one may experience the opening of the throat as a visceral, felt experience. It is important to note that in spiritual awakening we can experience a shift that affects our biology rather than just a shift of our values. This occurs as we fall out of sync with our conditioned selves and into sync with the Eternal Presence.

We want to cultivate the ability to be able to speak from the deepest Wisdom we have access to. This means giving yourself and your partner the space to take time before speaking and if necessary close the eyes to go deeper inside. The Old Paradigm expects a rapid response to questions, but this is insane. If the question is worth asking, then the reply is worth waiting for. In this way, we gift ourselves with the chance to dig for the more subtle voice of the Soul within rather than speaking from the automatic, conditioned response of the ego. Trust your Truth is valid and important, even sacred. That being said, you don't owe anyone your Truth. Open up the space for yourself to speak your Truth and speak only when space is there to listen.

WHEN TO LET PAIN SPEAK?

The ideal we are reaching for is to be able to access and speak our Truth without being taken over by emotional charge, however, this takes a great deal of practice, so practice!

We heard in Chapter 6 of the practice - 'Cushion Talk' - in which strong emotional charge can be neutralized in a safe, conscious space, but some may be confused about where speaking your Truth ends and speaking from your emotions begins. Remember, you are *not* your emotions, you are something deeper. The entire Universe is in flux including your emotions, but *you* don't want to be in flux! You want to be grounded in the changeless Peace of your true nature, the best seat in the Kosmos.

That said, there may be times along the journey when it is healthy, necessary even, to speak from your emotions if that's where the consciousness is trapped in that particular relationship dynamic in that particular moment. Your particular personality structure plays a part. Is your personality gentle? Then learn to be fierce! Is your personality fierce? Then learn to be gentle! In this way the lamb learns it has within it the power of a lion and the lion learns it conceals beyond its ferocity, the gentle heart of a lamb.

JABBERING

Jabbering is space-filling, through repetitive, unconscious chatter. Jabbering is being afraid to be in the Presence, the power of its Silence and stillness and ability to expose all that is not in complete integrity with the highest Self. Jabbering is verbalizing most every thought your mind produces. Jabbering can be an unconscious habit passed down from a long line of jabberers. In extreme cases, jabbering can continue even when the person is on their own.

Even if your partner has a habit of jabbering, give your full attention, at least try it. When the full, unadulterated awareness of the entire Universe is attentively listening, the waves of the chattering mind are soon softened and before you know it you may find that you are in Presence together.

In a conscious relationship, we must find a way to relish dwelling in the Presence together. There's nothing more profound or healing than to enter into Silence together because there is nothing more precious than the Presence. It is from this place the Heart speaks.

Replace Jabbering with *Japa*

If you are the one that's jabbering and you catch yourself, half the battle is already won! Consider adopting a meditation practice known as *japa*, which is a Sanskrit word. To practice *japa* repeat a *mantra* (a high vibrational set of syllables or invocation) silently to yourself on the inside. Introduce your *mantra* at such times when it is necessary to calm and purify the mind. This is a powerful practice which many spiritual masters have advocated as a 'one-stop-shop' to Spiritual Enlightenment. Ultimately, this is because God is 'in' the mantra, that is to say, the vibration of the mantra matches the vibration of the Heart and so when repeated one's awareness is being focused and drawn inward toward the Source of creation itself.

If you don't have a *mantra*, we the authors have printed one on page 125 as well as the story of its origin. It is a *mantra* that is soothing for the Soul.

ADDRESS YOUR PARTNER'S HIGHEST SELF

Always speak from the Heart to the Heart. Avoid canvassing your partner's false self for opinions, particularly about others. As a rule of thumb, does what you are wanting to say feel divisive in any way, even subtly so? Or will what you're about to say, bring unity? Do not address your partner's ego. The further you walk down the Esoteric Path of Marriage, the more you will begin to glimpse the divine in your partner. All too aware of the pain of the ego you will want to uphold its dominance no more. Eventually, you will hardly see him or her as an 'I-dentity' but more and more as the Eternal Presence itself! Until this reality truly dawns as a felt and ecstatic, lived experience or knowing we simply do our best to be respectful of each other's consciousness, never demanding it as some sort of right but humbly requesting it.

"WHAT'S WRONG?"

If your partner seems taken under by something asking "What's wrong?", may not be the best approach in a conscious relationship. This is because the question is already loaded with a problem and so it invites story and may even hook your partner's mind sufficiently to create a story when they are trying hard to weather a negative/destructive 'thought-storm'. Asking a closed question such as 'Are you Okay?' would be better. From a place of total Compassion, you may sometimes be able to usefully ask: "Have you been believing thoughts?", or something of this ilk. Similarly, if your partner seems lost in thought, their eyes staring vacantly ahead, you may be able to bring awareness by gently saying something like: "What's thinking you?" Experiment with your language to see what works and what invites more duality; and continue to create space to strengthen your intuition.

ELIMINATE CONTROL LANGUAGE

Begin to eliminate words like 'should' that infringe on one another's free will. It's a good idea to tidy up the language and usage that we have inherited where there may be vestiges of the Old Paradigm, of subtle control or even manipulation. Instead, practice making your language precise and articulating your feelings accurately. Instead of, for example, "You should read this book, it's great.", consider something like "I love this book. I think you'd love it also."

HONOR YOUR AWARENESS

Realize, your consciousness is your own and you are never obligated to give it to anyone, no matter how strong the convention is to the contrary. Practice honoring your awareness in your partnership then slowly we will bring more awareness into the World.

Practice this affirmation: My Awareness is My Own. I May Give it to You Freely but don't You dare try to Take it from Me!

How many times have we found ourselves dis-empowered by answering questions from 'the Interrogator' that it didn't feel right to answer? In the Old Paradigm encouraging children to go against themselves to answer foolish questions from the unconscious mind of an elder is rife. It's why we lose our instinct about 'who' to trust who not to trust. When to speak when not to speak. Which energy to give our attention to. We know as little ones but it is conditioned out of us in the Old Paradigm and we need to re-learn it all.

In the New Paradigm, we learn not to demand attention or words from another being as a natural right but respectfully address the Being without being attached to whether or not we get a response or get the kind of response we want.

Remember Silence is also a valid form of communication. This is a major shift to under take for the human species! But make it we will make it we must! For in the Old Paradigm, if someone requests your attention, your attention is socially demanded, an answer to a question, mandatory in the most serious way. Failure to respond or give your attention may evoke deep-rooted societal outrage. The ego is demanding your attention! *Answer or I will commit violence upon you or have you hauled away by the authorities!*

A new, enlightened culture is wanting to be born through us, through our relationships in which consciousness is respected, intuition heightened and Compassion, commonplace.

By the same token, try not to speak idly. In a conscious relationship consider that you are requesting your partners full Eternal Presence and divinity every time you ask for their attention. With this in mind, not every thought needs to be given reality or verbalized. Make it conscious, what you share, and when to share it.

ELIMINATING UNCONSCIOUS SPEECH PATTERNS

Because our unconscious speech patterns are unconscious, our partner may notice them before we do. These may include 'umms', 'ahhs', 'yer knows', 'likes, and 'stuff like thats', and so many others. We can help one another to fine tune our communication if we so choose. Other unconscious speech patterns may come up only in specific situations like when we are around our family of origin or when we are using the telephone. Swearing or cussing can also be an unconscious pattern. Lead your partner by example in these instances and if you are going to assist your partner in letting go of an unconscious speech pattern do so gently. It can be uncomfortable to realize you are saying something or doing something without awareness. Nervous laughter can also be a way of covering pain and running away from the moment.

MASKS AND LITTLE WHITE LIES

Pay attention to your levels of honesty with your partner. If you notice you are sometimes resorting to little white lies, become interested in why you are not telling the absolute truth. If you are lying, if even in a small way there is fear or mistrust there. It may be something about your relationship dynamic that needs adjusting and/or it may be left over from a parental relationship in which as a child you lied to protect yourself from your parent's disapproval.

Or if you are the recipient of the little white lies from your partner you may wish to examine why you're being lied to. This stuff may be hard to spot and difficult to root out, buried amid the power dynamic.

OM NAMAH SIVAYA

See if this works for you. When engaged in a spiritual marriage or relationship to which both have agreed to devote to Self-Realization, Spiritual Enlightenment or personal growth we want to maintain a reverential, meditative vibration in the home because you never know, in any one given moment (until you develop supreme subtlety) how deeply within your partner may be. Therefore, we have found it useful to utter the mantra 'Om Namah Sivaya' to alert the other that we are about to speak to them instead of just blurting out a question or request or a "hey you". It is particularly useful to preface necessary communication to your partner during meditation or rousing your partner from sleep with an 'Om Namah Sivaya' (or something akin).

We also sometimes utter this mantra in place of 'please' and 'thank you' or to gently bring the other back to the Truth if necessary. We have found that it promotes Unity and Peace - for it minimizes use of the word 'you', which separates and is non-jarring to the Soul because of its high vibration. The *mantra* can be translated in many ways. 'Salutations to the Truth' is one translation, or 'I Bow Down to the Pure Consciousness of your True Nature' or even 'Greetings to the Cosmic Dancer Within You!'

It may even be useful to sincerely repeat this *mantra* out loud at a time when your partner has been completely overcome by a strong emotion like rage.

Again if you choose to adopt this practice, you can choose your own *mantra*, phrase or approach to best support this delicate process of transformation to which you are committed.

BANTER

In a worldly relationship, particularly when it's new there may be playful banter and flirtation. This often gets carried over into a long-term relationship. What starts this way can, in time, become more barbed that is to say, more of an exchange of pain as both parties attempt to hide the marital pain-body behind humorous inter-play. On the Esoteric Path of Marriage, exchange loaded banter for truthful communication and 'shun sarcasm completely'[10] for it adds a layer of artifice we don't need and is usually divisive. *Playful* banter, as an expression of joy is something else, it is only that we never want to replace sarcasm with sincerity.

TREADING ON EGG SHELLS?

On the Esoteric Path of Marriage, each partner must feel that they can express themselves fully and speak their truth without fear of offending, upsetting or angering their partner.

---

[10] Anandamayi Ma

In many households in the Old Paradigm, the biggest pain-body tends in its own, subtle way to rule the roost. Don't let this happen in your enlightened relationship.

Notice how much you censure your truth. Do you steer away from it in order to avoid conflict? If so, some fear has crept into your relationship dynamic, an imbalance that needs to be addressed so that you can both become your most powerful, conscious, sovereign selves.

If however you feel yourself sensitive (in the midst of all of this honest communication) as though your partner is tearing into you by drawing attention to your egoic patterns and such like, first consider what 'you' it is that considers itself to be torn into. That which you really are is untouchable. If need be, you could always speak to your partner and let them know you are feeling sensitive and ask them not to censure themselves but to be a bit more gentle on you.

BABY TALK

For some couples, baby-talk can be a flip-side of a dominant/submissive-type dynamic and so it may seem a welcome respite for one or other. But what we're seeking is to free ourselves of all such dynamics, and rest in perfect balance with ourselves, and in relation to one another; and so tidying up these little communication quirks by getting to the root of them can be powerfully renewing. Often those affected by baby-talk hardly know they're doing it!

For those determined to birth their mature, sovereign Selves, make it conscious and watch it fall away! However, if you and your partner do have a genuinely balanced relationship and simply enjoy the play of baby-talk, don't let us stop you! All must be free to express and play! Only make sure it's not covering up some deeper feelings or being used in subtle manipulation.

PET NAMES? MAKE THEM CONSCIOUS!

Hold a high vision for your partner and be willing to let pet names that have surpassed their usefulness be replaced by new monikers that uphold your partner's Divine Self. Terms of endearment such as "Babe" or "Baby" may ultimately also be outgrown by the relationship. Do you want your partner to remain small and cute or recognize his/herself as an Empowered Presence?

CALLING BETWEEN ROOMS, A GOOD IDEA?

The practice of holding long-range conversation with your partner, calling or shouting your thoughts or questions from room to room or down the stairs may not be suitable on the Esoteric Path of Marriage. Though seemingly practical we do not know how deep a meditative space our partner may be in or what kind of focused activity they may be involved in. Also, one can grow hoarse and frustrated calling and we may not hear the reply anyway making for more frustration. Perhaps if you have something to say, it is worth walking to your partner to address them directly, which can also cut back on general household noise pollution, making for a more peaceful living environment.

Wishing You Clear, Joyful, Sincere, Heartfelt Commune-ication!

8. PRACTICAL WAYS TO PROMOTE HARMONY & UNITY

MEDITATION

A daily meditation practice, ideally together, is the bedrock of the Esoteric Path of Marriage. Meditating together will harmonize your subtle bodies and promote harmony between your forms. Support one another in this, always leading by example rather than by cajoling.

When confusion, fear, anger or doubt is taking you over, let meditation be your knight in shining armor. The Heart can process emotions thousands of times faster than the mind so we can get into the habit of solving all worldly woes and marital disharmony through meditation. Only after the emotional charge has been cleared or transmuted does clarity naturally arise. After meditation, you may not even need to talk about it.

Which Meditation Technique?

There are many ways to meditate through guided online meditations, to visualizations, to gazing at a flame with a soft focus, to *mantra*-based meditations or the use of binaural tapes and glasses, etc.

Choose a technique that you can be doing whenever and wherever you are. This is because we want to leave room for our practice to evolve from what begins as a once or twice-daily 'practice' into eventually, a moment-by-moment lived experience of our Selves.

The most profound meditation techniques are those that allow one to enter the dimension of feeling since this is a powerful way to dismantle the mental, emotional and pain bodies. We will share with you below the technique that has been at the heart of our spiritual awakening and our relationship.

The Technique

First, use a *mantra* to focus the mind or watch your breath or both at the same time.

Then become aware of subtle sensations within yourself and allow your consciousness to 'dance' from sensation to sensation, like a butterfly moving from flower to flower. If a more technical explanation speaks to you, use the focus of the Mind's Eye, the kinesthetic felt-sense and directional focus of the brain to 'scan' the body for sensations.

The sensation of sound, both gross and subtle, can also be included as a sensation to feel and listen to. Don't forget to feel the wind too.

If we become absorbed in thoughts, we can bring ourselves gently back to either the *mantra* or the breath and the dimension of feeling.

The surface-mind's stream of consciousness can also be observed as something separate from one, hence entering the Witness State.

The Mantra

(We offer this mantra for personal use to anyone who feels drawn to its vibration.)

Through Kundalini Awakening brought on by an intense meditation practice, I, David began spontaneously expressing syllables which later turned into words, primarily in Sanskrit but other languages also and primarily names of God. Eventually, full mantras would express through me, sometimes even in song - melodies foreign to my mind. I say 'express through me' because the Presence of Being-ness is so strong at these times that there is no premeditation of thought just an expression from the depths of the source of ones existence.

One specific *mantra* that came through from this place beyond mind and time we share with you here. Follow its vibration back to your Heart and allow its vibration to reverberate silently there during meditation. This *mantra,* as with many, is not meant to be spoken out loud except perhaps when first practicing the *mantra.*

Mu Hara Ma Namaha

'Mu' means to be on the very edge of something, as in a body of water; to be close to final liberation. 'Hara' is God/Shiva/The Eternal Presence. 'Ma' is Divine Love and 'Namaha' is 'I bow down'. Thus the mantra translates as follows:

On the Banks of the River of Spiritual Liberation, I bow Down to Love.

HEALING ONE ANOTHER

It will ease the relationship greatly to have a method of healing one another. It builds Compassion and Unity, especially after a 'mind storm' or pain-body feeding-frenzy. You could both receive a Reiki attunement to 'open up the channels', the healing energy that flows works really well with massage. If you choose to learn Reiki, find a sincere practitioner to perform your attunement who meditates daily and is pure-living. What a sweet way of bonding in Spirit to gently lay hands on one another's bodies in trying times.

In your spiritual practice perhaps your own method of healing will arise but Reiki is a beautiful way to begin to bestow healing and it will restore radical peace between the two of you. We the authors quite naturally developed ways of flowing constant healing between our forms back and forth through techniques that spontaneously arose.

Feeding one another

Who can be angry with the one that they feed and who can be angry with the one that feeds them?

Feeding your partner can reset your relationship to the pure dynamic between mother and child otherwise known as Unconditional Love.

Do this with absolute Presence and Patience and you will soon feel the love spring back into your Hearts once more.

Heart-to-heart feeling meditation

Lie one on top of the other, naked or clothed, lightest one on top or whichever way is most comfortable. (If you are unable to lie like this for any reason, you can get a similar effect by lying tightly together on your sides.) Close the eyes and rest in this comforting position. Become very present. Feel the gentle rise and fall of your chests as breathing occurs. Feel the warmth in your Heart centers. Perhaps you will be able to feel the flow of subtle energy flowing between the two Hearts.

Once a steady connection between the Heart centers is observed, become aware of your solar plexus, belly, groins and feet resting together. Feel into, observe and enjoy the flow of energy and flow of sensation between the two forms. Notice the flow of Love from organ to organ on your physical bodies as your bodies begin to 'talk' the only language they know, the language of Love, reciprocity and healing.

Sexual arousal may occur, is it any different from this language of Love, reciprocity and healing?

This can be done last thing before going to sleep at night, first thing in the morning or as a precursor to love-making.

Head-to-head meditation

Lying or sitting, hold hands and bring your foreheads together so that they are touching and notice the flow of healing and harmonization between your heads. It may feel good to move your foreheads to create a massage effect as thoughts and sensations, stored in the cellular memory, get released. Put all your attention into your foreheads and into your brains and minds. Notice the mind gets calm and the brain feel soothed. You will soon feel like you are of one mind and may get 'bliss-brain'.

TIME APART - ACCEPT AND ENJOY

Sometimes each may be called to stand alone, apart

from the other. Maybe you hit a crisis point in the relationship where the only way through is to give yourself space. Or maybe circumstances beyond the control of the 'person' intervene to force a separation for your own goods. It need not be a problem, it's your chance to expand and deepen on your own. When you come back together, what a gift you will be to your partner! Wiser, stronger and more grounded in yourself. Don't take on the story of the Old Paradigm where separation spells PROBLEM, FAILURE, DIVORCE. Conscious Separation is something quite different.

Time apart was even predicted for us by an esteemed Vedic Astrologer Sri Mohan of Amritapuri in India. Eventually, the time arrived when circumstances and feelings seemed to be pulling us in two different directions. David went to the USA to begin my, Maha's visa process and I stayed in England, each of us reckoning we'd be back together within about 3 months at most. Saying our farewells at the airport we were both deeply present with our feelings and hugging, we both wept. In that embrace of fully-felt emotion, it was as though our Hearts had healed one another and we were able to separate without looking back and enjoy the new ride.

One year later we were finally reunited and were surprised when our reunion uncovered feelings of grief at having denied ourselves the bliss of being together for so long. We had both thrown ourselves deeply into spiritual practices that year and when we came back together there was a strangeness neither could have predicted for we had evolved perhaps eons in the interim (meditation effectively speeds up one's evolution) and even our faces were subtly different. We expected instant joy, but it unearthed more complex emotions, collective even, giving us both the feeling that we were in some way acquiring the empathy for the grief of those separated for long periods due to war and such like.

It also struck us both how pointless the Skype conversations had been, which only synthesized our being together. Within minutes grief gave way to elation. The reunion experience was for us both a highly treasured, emotionally rich experience. And following this separation the new light we'd each mined separately combusted into deeper levels of spiritual ripening together.

SOUL-GAZING

A favorite meditation of ours and one that at certain periods of our *sadhana* has been our primary practice.

Get so that you are physically very close to each other, comfortably facing each other. Connect to your Heart and gaze into your partner's eyes. Look beyond all labels (e.g. names, wife/husband/partner, woman/man, person, etc.). Let most of your awareness sink into your Heart center so that you are not looking at your partner with 'hard' eyes but with a 'soft gaze'. Feel whatever arises with equanimity. See whatever arises with equanimity. Commune as deeply as you are able, without judgment. Look with your Heart, not your eyes.

THE BIG OM

I Maha took up this practice after seeing the translation of a Sanskrit *bhajan* (in an *ashram*) written by an Indian sage. One of the lines read: *Chant the sacred syllable OM like a mad-man until you reach the Supreme Goal!* I started OMming on my own for long periods to clear myself out during times of emotional turbulence. Then we began a practice of OMming together and eventually began sharing the Big OM with groups.

Chant the sacred syllable 'OM' from the depths of yourselves. Merge in the sound together. Become the witness of the sound that is being produced. Other sounds may express other than OM; the intelligence of your being knows very well exactly what sound it needs to produce to bring healing. Note, the 'MMM' sound can be as important as the 'OOO' sound, and has its own healing function, feel it reverberate through your sinuses, brain, etc. No need to OM in exact unison (timing each OM together as in a *yoga* class) instead let it be free-form so that your body can breathe when it needs to. Observe any thoughts being produced alongside the OM, let them pass through you or be swept away by the OM. As you go deep, your body may naturally begin to move therapeutically as it unwinds tension, let yourself be free.

No one really needs to learn this practice, it's pretty much what you came into this world doing, feeling deeply and letting rip in sound. This, though you're able to use your voice in a more sophisticated way and enjoy the natural harmonies and dissonances that are created with other voices.

OM like this for 5 to 10 minutes to clear your mind or

OM for 30-40 minutes (or longer) to feel yourself vibrating in the Silence.

As with all deep meditations, it's good to lay down for five minutes or so afterwards in relaxation. Such deep healing to your Mind, Heart and Soul and such a feeling of Unity will be exposed. This practice clears the cobwebs out faster than silent meditation. OM in the car, OM as you prepare the food, OM for the Joy of it! (Why not start your own Big OM events and spread this powerful practice far and wide?)

You may also burst into OM at any moment that Unity needs to be restored. Don't OM identified with pain but enter Presence and OM from there with the intention of helping to clear the layers away, maybe your partner will view it as an invitation for healing and join you. What fuel is OM for the Esoteric Path of Marriage!

SACRED DANCE
(AKA Dancing By Yourself, Together)

In the Old Paradigm, we dance from the outside rather than from within. We have learnt to dance for others, which can be fun but doesn't put us in touch with our

Bliss. We have learnt to dance to a beat, moving our bodies in time to a rhythm. Sacred Dance is something different.

Communing with the vibration of the sound, we close our eyes to open up space within, to make space within for the music. Organically we match its patterning and we find we are moving; the music itself seems to be moving us. We feel the heat of the Earth's energy winding up through our feet. We commune with the music through the feeling-tone of our own being allowing our Souls to embrace our bodies.

If our body dances it is beyond our effort as we are danced by the Source of Music itself; we dance *with* the Source of Music itself.

We may enter states of Bliss and Joy in our dance, we may cry and laugh touching ever-new dimensions within. The music being a key, to enter doors beyond even the music itself. Any music which invites you into a feeling-tone will do. Music that resonates with the depths of our Lives. It will be different for everyone, but it is the music of Truth.

LOVE-MAKING

What an exquisite gift is ours to restore unity, Love and

understanding in our relationships and Joy to our Hearts. Whilst love-making in the Old Paradigm can be a painful tug between resistance and wanting, in the New Paradigm we make it a safe place to unburden fears, pains and confusion and it becomes a vehicle for Compassion, Bliss, Peace, Devotion and Unity thus taking us beyond the personal. For more on making sex your *sadhana,* see Chapter 10.

DIET

Enjoy raising your energy and creating healthy habits that serve the partnership and what it is dedicated to. Observe the way food makes you feel after you eat it and eat what feels good and boosts your vibrancy rather than going on taste alone.

Make it fun and creative to find new ways to eat healthily. Try eating light, a high percentage of raw (and organic where possible) and take enjoyment from the subtle creative energy (and 'highs') built from food. However let us also be practical and grateful for the food that is available to us without concern. It is said that eating a frozen pizza with Gratitude is better for one than consuming a super-food feast with disdain.

Let us be aware that there is consciousness in all our food, which is why in some cultures food is eaten in silence. By the same token, preparing food with Presence affects the consciousness of the food, as does preparing it with resentment or impatience or your mind on other things. Such is the subtle nature of reality!

TAKE REFUGE IN SILENCE

When circumstances are tough, when your emotional wounds are being prodded and poked, when every time you open your mouth you seem to be clashing with your partner's pain it may be time to take refuge in Silence. It's hard to quarrel with someone who's in Silence. It can be a good way to restore truthful communication, Patience and emotional processing to your relationship, not to mention Peace and connection to your Self. Most likely these periods of Silence will be exclusively in the safety of your partnership or like-minded community.

It can be tough if your partner is the one in silence especially if you are left to communicate for them but be supportive and enjoy the Peace.

As a spiritual practice, you could take it turns to be silent on alternate days, it will deepen your connection to one another as you will come to be grateful for your partner's Presence even if they are choosing not to speak.

PLAY

It is said that two people can build a bond with one another faster in one hour of play than in 20 hours of talking. We have found getting into the ocean brings us into Presence and returns us to joy. Anything that raises us up buoyantly above the Mundane. Some other suggestions are skiing, surfing, trampolining, frisbee, head-stands, dancing, music concerts, hanging upside down, hoola-hooping, camping and hiking in Nature! Any activity that brings you into Spirit or brings you into Presence with yourself. Surrender to your play; let your play become your meditation and your meditation become your play.

The Gratitude Game

It's pretty simple, come fair weather or come foul, you lie in bed taking it in turns to think of something you are grateful for and sharing it. By routinely returning yourselves to this vibration of Gratitude you may find a sublime Gratitude surfaces in your every day life for no reason at all, but for the Joy of existence.

Make use of what you do have and the gifts you have access to, and you will be given more.

Yes, the fruits of your destiny may be in the future but the seeds are surely of the vibration of the present moment.

The Monster Game

This is a fun, light-hearted game (if you enjoy this kind of play-acting) and is a great way to engender Compassion for monsterkind.

The monster snarls, grimaces, hisses and expresses its monsterhood in whatever way feels natural. The other faces the monster, looking upon it with the eyes of a loving mother until the monster's monsterousness is naturally humbled with Love and transformed into an innocent baby monster. No faking your Compassion! (Hint: once you can see through the filters in play with your partner (in this game or Soul-Gazing) it will help you to recognize your Beloved in other people, and everywhere.)

9. NAVIGATING THE LABYRINTH

As the last flames of the Old Paradigm rage, we must find a way to bridge the realms without falling through the cracks, getting burnt or giving up.

Don't blame yourselves if you find yourselves in terribly difficult circumstances. The challenge is often to hold a high vision and retain our perspective amid a world that persistently projects its own coding on to us and our situation. In a relationship, we have a golden opportunity to help one another navigate and hold the space to nurture our deepest truths.

But the structure of the Old Paradigm, governed by the monetary system produces many challenges, Catch 22s and seeming paradoxes, with its own views on marriage and relationship. Hold steady! Remember each and every one of us is in the midst of a paradigm shift, therefore the rules of old no longer apply to us.

Here we share some practical approaches for transcending the Mundane of the old as we enter the living Now and the new.

MONEY

In the Old Paradigm, we experience a problem related to work or money, and we feel very stressed. Money-worries in the Old Paradigm strangle a person. It can be like struggling for air to breathe and indeed money or lack thereof has played a factor in many a suicide. Being without it or having the possibility of being without it is akin to the threat of death; it evokes primal fear. It is in this context that money, associated with Life itself, is venerated in place of God (Love).

Since in the Old Paradigm money and work are inextricably linked, issues and problems around work and the work place are a big source of anxiety. When they hit, the way of the Old Paradigm is to worry and even despair, to let these vibrations drive one to thrash about for compromises and make rash decisions because in the Old Paradigm fear precludes the existence of an empty space or even the prospect of an empty space.

In the New Paradigm a 'problem' surfaces and it is information from some part of ourselves. If it is work or purpose-related, it may be an indication that what we are doing is no longer serving our highest good or the highest good of the Whole. Perhaps it is a clue that a dynamic needs adjusting. If it is money related, it may indicate a holding back of our gifts and talents from the World. Or it could be that our consciousness is still being cultivated *through* the 'problem' for some specific gift or talent, being perfected within, yet to be fully born.

Whatever the source of the 'problem', it is a teacher and a guide, an invitation to step into the Mystery. We may still feel the stress and anxiety rising within, with its story, but we do not let these negativities move us. Instead, we understand everything comes out of consciousness so every problem can be solved from the root level of consciousness.

We try to cultivate the Trust and Strength to inhabit the empty space wherein something may have died and the new thing may not yet have become visible. Meditation is your ally. From there we are in tune with the Universal Mind and solutions from the quantum computer within will come. All we need do is be brave and be open to receiving them in the myriad ways Existence speaks to us. From here we can act but it will be a very different action than would have been performed from the vibration of fear.

The important thing is to know your priorities. We may have fooled ourselves in the Old Paradigm thinking of money as having some sort of virtue but in actuality, in and of itself, money has no virtue and no inherent values. The priorities of the Old Paradigm are to have plenty of money (at any cost) but in the New Paradigm it is the quality of ones consciousness at any one given moment that really matters; out of this true productivity and prosperity is birthed.

In the New Paradigm, actions are not performed exclusively for money. For the time being, since as a collective we are somewhere between the Old and the New, some of our actions may be performed exclusively for money, but they should at least be actions that allow us to be ourselves, and actions that do not require us to go against our integrity, actions that are acceptable to us.

Some actions though they are 'moral' from an old

paradigm perspective (because they are putting food on the table) may actually be damaging in some larger way. It's no longer enough just to be a good provider for the sake of it, for now we take into consideration how our action and worldly duties affect the Whole that we are a part of. Indeed, we *are* the Whole, we are not only a 'part' of it! As each of us contains the Whole, we are each the center of the Whole Universe, which has no circumference! Therefore in the New Paradigm we look to provide solutions to problems, following our Heart's calling and inspiration instead of looking to a busy-ness that provides money for the sake of money but may leave us unfilled in Spirit or feeling damaged in some way. It may be providing no apparent benefit and perhaps even a worldly destruction. Hence money for money's sake is not the goal but rather, money is more of a by-product of certain things we do, there is a difference of motivation. In certain cases, it takes only a switch of attitude. An action may seem humdrum, or pointless on the grand scale but bring your Presence and your Love and your acceptance to the action and suddenly God is working through you.

Money is a temporary structure, it has not always been here and will one day become obsolete as we each undergo a shift of consciousness, stepping into the Joy of creating, giving and problem-solving to make the World a better place; but not before money has itself been 'enlightened' through us. We enlighten money by making Love our bottom line.

As an aside, during a transition period one may also find it useful to consider what the *Vedic* Astrologer in India said to us:

"Karmically it's more important how you spend your money than how you earn it."

PURPOSE

Many are concerned that they don't know what their purpose is or their calling to serve the Whole has not yet revealed itself. Your true purpose is to Wake Up, that is to say to encourage yourself to new depths of Presence in every moment, new vibrational heights within. Awakening itself will reveal the opportunities in which you can serve the World. Gifts bubble up from Love and things you love to do and sometimes those things in which there is an apparent deficiency is a clue to a hidden gift or spiritual purpose waiting to be alchemized.

If you are in a partnership, use it to your collective advantage and work together as a team to support one another in following and trusting each other's highest calling and truth. Have reverence for each other's gifts, which may well be complementary to your own. If one of you is aligned with your work and the other is not, then support the one who is not to find liberation. Help one another to draw yourselves to your Loves, not your fears.

MATERIALISM

After an awakening remember you have the option to simplify your life, if need be, rather than struggle to maintain a job that calls you to go against your ideals or no longer suits your expanding consciousness, new perspective, and heightened sensitivity. Your relationship to yourself and, therefore, the whole Kosmos may have entirely shifted; this is no small thing!

Resist any temptation to compare your lives to those

in the Old Paradigm. Hence: forget about the Jonsies! On an *ashram* wall in Southern India, there is written an Indian proverb, which with contemplation can switch your synapses and set you free from the conditioning of materialism that is so liberally applied in the Old Paradigm. The proverb reads:

"Multiply your wants, live like a beggar; reduce your wants, live like a King."

IN THE FIRE

All your 'stuff' is being brought up, your partnership is in disarray, the path ahead looks frightening or unclear and despair is knocking on your door. Is this the time to sit down and make plans or evaluate your relationship and your life? No, first get yourself calm and neutralize the emotional charge. Enter the Presence and allow It to be compassionate and loving towards that part of you that feels it is losing control. Clarity and inspiration are always bubbling up from within yet this can only be realized when the waters of the mind are calm and clear.

Make No Plans From a Low Vibration!

Through the filters of the ego and the Old Paradigm a situation can seem terrible, but without the filters that exact same situation can be a graceful blessing. In addition, the myriad false selves of others around you may think your situation is a disaster when you see the Grace and Beauty of it; it's part of the challenge of Waking Up, to learn to navigate these judgments and projections without letting them affect us. There are many levels of reality, "many mansions in my Father's home", as Jesus said.

And remember you are dying and being reborn simultaneously so be compassionate with yourselves and trust that whatever is happening, each moment is uniquely designed to bring us ever-closer to realization of our *true nature*.

When a caterpillar enters into the process of metamorphosis, there is a stage at which, within the chrysalis there is only liquid. At this stage, there is no caterpillar and there is no sign of a butterfly either. You both may be going through this process simultaneously and so your relationship may at times, resemble this kind of apparent decimation to those looking on.

However take heart! Be strong and give up blame, have heroic faith in the (super)natural process that is happening within you. If you are going through this with a partner, building the kind of relationship that is reciprocally supportive to genuine Spiritual Growth, consider yourselves Lucky! Your relationship will ultimately also be of benefit to others.

ENVIRONMENTS

Be extra aware when you enter the space of others. If you visit friends who have a heavy marital pain-body have the stealth and awareness of a tiger lest you yourselves become the pain of those particular vibrations. Remember, it is not exclusively their pain, it is a vibration. Have you ever noticed how quickly you may begin to clash with your partner if another couple you are with is at war? If you are with the warring couple and you don't have the kind of dynamic where you can hold space for them or bring healing, then consider leaving them to it. If you do have that relationship, perhaps you could suggest a group Big OM session.

"No problem can be solved from the same level of consciousness that created it." - Albert Einstein

More broadly, you may come to notice how the feeling-tone of an environment you enter is *causally related* to the output of your mind. These thoughts may seem personal because they pertain to your life-circumstances but are only being produced in that moment because they match a certain vibration in the ether you are passing through.

PRAYER

One does not beseech a reluctant or capricious God to give us what we want. That's the Old Paradigm projecting its own perspective on to the *Kosmos*. Instead, build a relationship with the *Presence* of God accessible through your own Heart. Give all your fears, worries and doubts to that eternal, unconditionally loving conscious Beingness, which ultimately you are not separate from.

Raise your vibration through your inner arts practices so that you can merge into this Presence and receive the blessings and insights that are being given from the abundance of the Universal Mind, 100% of the time in every direction.

Inwardly ask for guidance, solutions, healing or to see a way through, the response may be quick, so be watchful for it. Once your relationship with the I AM Presence is firmly established your pure intention becomes a prayer and a blessing to anything you bring your attention to. It is a dance, a knowing, and an understanding all beyond words.

TRAGEDY

"A Full and Powerful Soul not only copes with painful even terrible losses, deprivations, robberies, insults; it emerges from such hells with a Greater Fullness and Powerfulness, and Most Essential of all with a New Increase in the Bliss-Fullness of Love."

- Nietzsche, *The Will To Power*

Sometimes as a partnership you may face cataclysmic events and happenings, which can tear at the heart of a marriage. Each story is unique but all such unfoldings present similar challenges. Challenges to our perspective, our Peace, our Faith, our Love, our loyalty (to Truth), our Compassion (to ourselves) and the strength of our spiritual practice and understanding. If both partners are undergoing dramatic challenges of these kinds, simultaneously a relationship may find itself in crisis.

However, the relationship may also be significantly deepened just as each individual may be significantly deepened by 'the worst thing' happening. To that degree, every tragedy has a divine purpose - however hard to see from the midst of it - that involves an element of sacrifice in order to gain lessons that may not be wrought in any other way.

These events dredge up a cocktail of (often contradictory) richly-felt emotions, which in turn produce such thoughts as:

- This should not be happening or this should not have happened (Fighting with what is)
- What is happening is bad and not good, this episode is an exception to the laws of nature, somehow we have diverged from 'God's Plan' (Loss of Faith)
- This is my fault. (Guilt)
- God/Life has abandoned me. (Anger towards God/Life)
- God/Life has betrayed me. (Victim-hood)
- I am living in a hostile Universe that doesn't love me. (Despair)

Are you able to be present with your partner in the face of tragedy? Can you hold their hand, so to speak, and go with them, into the darkness? It may be abhorrent to look upon, almost impossible to face. However, we can come through this with Presence, Bravery, and Compassion. Is your partner emotionally falling apart? Then hold the Space.

We the authors came through one such cataclysm ourselves. I Maha recall a grief and an anguish so deep that going into the feelings induced a panic, a sort of suffocation, as though I would die from such pain.

David was able to be Present with me during this Dark Night of the Soul (though the tragedy that prompted it was also his) and serve me in such a way that I still feel the gratitude and still hold the learning. Amidst feelings of unfathomable anguish and hours of weeping, I reached a threshold of emotional feeling over which I was terrified to step. He fearlessly went into the pain with me; he knew through the deeply empathic relationship that we have, that I was on the brink and he said: "I know you are feeling like you can hardly stand another moment of this pain but go into it, I'm going into with you."

Like a surgeon of consciousness he said: "I promise you, the intensity of this anguish will not last long." I gripped his hand and together we went where 'Angels Fear to Tread', so to speak. In moments, having crossed the threshold of hell, the anguish I had been running from diminished like a shadow brought to light as it was touched by our collective consciousness.

We can promise you, for us both, the unmanageable horror and grief never did return with the same intensity. It was vanquished that night.

When the grief/horror is at its height one has the pain and one is in the grip of the *fear* of the pain. Charging your Presence heroically into it, dropping story, not only alchemizes your pain but simultaneously rids you of the fear of it. Now you can take a breath once more. Now your mind is receptive to the Grace that is wanting to flow into you in the form of ways to understand and yes, make peace with the tragedy, the *Kosmic* perspective if you will. For when one has fully accepted the pain of it, one is no longer holding ones fists up to Reality but has ones arms and chest thrown open to It, and from here, understanding, solutions, insights, healing comes flooding in from all four corners of the Universe to crown the hero at the apex of his journey; the Dragon is slain.

In the wake of such a journey, one is left with the process of watching the mind and its habitual need to get one to re-live the most horrifying moments. Accept any pictures associated with the horror/grief/fear that may appear in your mind's eye, don't push them away but don't run towards them either. Let them pass so as they don't become you. During this process, you will also be carefully dis-identifying from the key thoughts (such as the thoughts bullet-pointed a little earlier in this section).

As the intensity simmers down from boiling point over the ensuing days, weeks and months be vigilant as the Victim pain-body attempts to feed. It can be surprising how seductive the pain-body is that wants to make an identity out of tragedy. Ultimately, though you may waver and weaken many times, it hurts too much to be reduced to a painful story. Thus, beware whom you spend time with in the fall-out of tragedy, beware other people's mind-projections. They may not be prepared for just how fast and how thoroughly you can heal and become ever more expansive in Spirit; with a beautiful perspective, Courage, Compassion, and a determination not to be made small by the experiences that flow through you, as the unconscious within you attempts to make itself conscious.

The practices in the Esoteric Path of Marriage are here for you whether the seas are stormy or calm.

God Bless You Warriors of Truth!

10. OPENING PANDORA'S BOX

In the myth, Pandora is the first woman and her name means "All Gifts". Prometheus has bestowed the gift of fire on Man (a metaphor for the Fire of Transformation or the *Kundalini*). This he has done without Zeus's permission, angering the Gods. As a kind of *karmic* repercussion for this action, Zeus orders Hephaestus to create Pandora and give her to Prometheus' brother Epimetheus as a bride. She is given along with a locked box (and a key), which she is told never to open.

She intends to play by Zeus's rules, but the box calls to her in such a way that she decides to open it, releasing death, pain, and sorrow upon the World. She believes she has done something terrible and closes it hurriedly before the last of its contents can be released, the Light of Hope. Eventually, the Light calls to her also and she must trust her own feelings and dare to open the box one more time.

Through the filters of the Old Paradigm that has a tendency to interpret Myth with a literal translation, opening Pandora's Box has come to denote a trifling, unwise action that leads to great destruction, the same as Eve's eating from the Tree of Knowledge. Our ancient forbears are seen in the Old Paradigm as naive and less intelligent and so their mythology is misinterpreted as simple stories trying to explain how we ended up with such things as death and fire and cautioning against curiosity.

However, Pandora's Box is a metaphor for all those things that we do not want to see (or feel), our contradictions, confusions and our emotional pain, which is intermingled with our Light and our Power. If we do not lift the lid of the box we cannot know who we really are; in lifting the lid of the box we need no longer be afraid of its contents.

SEX AS SADHANA

Our journeys led us to India and to the ancient *yogic* traditions on our path to Self-Realization. The ancient *yogic* scriptures advise against sex for those seeking union with God. For married people who are seeking Absolute Truth the tradition cautions against ego-based sexuality and instead advises a *yogic*, meditative approach.

But how do we engage in meditative, ego-free love-making if we discover that we and/or our partner has a sexual ego/sexual pain-body forged in the dying embers of the Old Paradigm, built on sexual exploitation, gender-wars, pornography, confusion, emotional avoidance and spiritual denial all born out of a mass-state of illusion, which we could call 'total mind-body identification', the underlying cause of human suffering in this World? How do we navigate this mine-field of our inner terrain together to benefit ourselves spiritually?

The reason the ancient *yogic* scriptures advise against sex is for two core reasons. First, because liberation is attained through dis-identification with form and identification with Spirit. These scriptures warn strongly against our *vasana*s or inherited tendencies towards bodily pleasure lest we get so distracted by the pleasure of the body that we never transcend. Therefore the *yogi* is to see pain and pleasure with equanimity, as sensations to be experienced but not run towards or run away from.

The second reason the *yogic* scriptures advise the yogi against sex is because the *yogi* is working with the *Kundalini*. The *Kundalini* is the feminine God-force, the Creative force behind Nature that lies latent within every human being for the purposes of evolution. When worked *with*, this spiritual energy is for the purpose of re-directing that force that is normally used to pro-create another human being, towards radical evolution of the species on the level of consciousness. This evolution will take the *yogi* from the self-aware state of realizing that he is a Human Being into a lived experience of himself as being one with the Eternal Presence itself. If this *Kundalini* energy is frittered away through the energetic release of orgasm, the *yogic* scriptures warn, then this profound Gift will not be reached.

So what is sex for, for those seeking the ultimate realization of the Self? Is it to be largely avoided or embraced?

The Esoteric Path of Marriage teaches the narrow way of freeing the Self through relationship and yes, even through *sex*.

The reader may be familiar with the word '*Tantra*'. In the West, it is largely synonymous with '*tantric*-sex' as a vehicle that will take your partnership towards more longer-lasting, more fulfilling love-making. It is geared towards non-goal orientated sex, promising waves of continual pleasure rather than building to or chasing (an often all-too-quick) orgasm.

Tantra in the East is, in fact, a (largely buried) spiritual path in and of itself, a path that recognizes the totality of the Being must be liberated, including the sexual side of the Being.

Traditionally a *Tantrika* would be sent to the *yogi* on the mountain-top once he'd reached a certain level of Enlightenment in order to help him complete his transcendence. A *Tantrika* is a female (the male form is called a *Tantrik*) who is no longer identified with form and is firmly established in Spirit. She is so deeply compassionate and intuitive that she offers up her own body to the *yogi* and guides him from her deepest, non-judging Self in order to free him from his various desires, aversions and perversions, because only then will he be truly free.

In the West, the sexual ego is complex and tricky to dismantle; in addition to millennia of patriarchy (which, of course, persists in the East also), strong conditioning in films, television and often early exposure to pornography[11] is combined with a bombardment of mixed messages from childhood onwards from a permissive yet repressive culture.

For the spiritual aspirant, there may be disassociation from the body due to a strong meditation practice but the desires, aversions and sometimes perversions are still holding parts of us. There may be buried shame and denial. After years of meditation, it might seem unpalatable and even scary for those who have been, through the *yogic* (or monastic) path conditioned against sex, especially since there may be a bunch of pain/ego wrapped up in it. We want to be 'pure' but our minds may hold stories of fantasies, desires and perversions that are incompatible with the holiness we are reaching for and so we can end up adding new layers to our ego of guilt and self-judgment.

---

[11] With the advent of the internet those in the East may also now be exposed early-on to pornography

In our relationship we the authors experienced an intricate confusion of aversion and attraction winding itself around and around into an elaborate, tight knot of pain and anguish that neither of us knew how to untie.

What I, David uncovered was a many-layered sexual false-self built of bravado, rejection, projection and the idea I had of what making love looked like from the perspective I had been exposed to of it, basically a submissive female led by the man. It was a lot of pressure and a source of anxiety.

From my, Maha's perspective it was as though a completely different entity took control of David - this was his default mode - when it came to sex and my energy could only be aroused by Spirit, not by ego. Complicating the set-up was David's (valid) concern about frittering away his *Kundalini* following the massive *Kundalini* Awakening he had experienced.

I Maha was unsure how to help steer our sexual relationship into healing. Previously, all of my sexual desire was hooked up to my ego, coming from a craving to have attention from men, (one of the conditioned effects of millennia of patriarchy) so when that piece fell away (quite instantaneously in my first spiritual awakening as I experienced myself at a deeper level) sex had no further draw for me. Quite the opposite; it was a confusion I wasn't ready to face and a pain I didn't want to explore. I was deepening spiritually, what did sex have to do with me? My setup was complicated by an acutely sensitive body to which David's conditioned self was unadjusted and unaccustomed. Intuitively I knew that my body was wired for higher sexuality but David was still mired in his conditioning and I remained aloof from it.

Thus, we were uniquely destined to largely avoid a sexual relationship during the first years of our awakenings until such a stage was reached when we were spiritually equipped to dismantle both our marital sexual pain-body and our individual sexual pain-bodies. We share these travails in order to show the arc that is possible from agony and avoidance to the heights of *Tantric* union with the ecstatic Self.

Though our minds had been prepared, for us, it can

hardly be said that we discovered *Tantra*; when we reached a certain stage, *Tantra* discovered us. In our case, though the esoteric experience is difficult to translate, a *Tantrika* opened up from the inside as we touched ever-deeper dimensions of reality within ourselves, to guide us boldly, fearlessly, unashamedly, and playfully through the jungle of our sexual impressions.

The most important thing to remember is to be Present. Due to our conditioning with its preoccupation with outward appearance and 'sexiness' there is a strong tendency for us to go 'out of body' and into our heads during love-making. Women think they have to be a porn-star (at least in the West) and men think they have to be dynamite lovers who can go all night, both of which take one into an idea of oneself, adding extra layers of 'performance'. Thus in the Old Paradigm love-making brings us more heavily into duality, building ego. It can become the opposite of making love.

Also, truthful communication, sharing what is presenting itself within you is important, as is establishing a safe non-judging space to liberate ourselves in and dive deep into feeling.

Finding new language and new understanding for what sex is *for*, for those on a spiritual path can be liberating. For example rather than using language like 'turning each other on', which may contain feelings of confusion for those on the spiritual path (whom is getting turned on, is it the ego?), consider that your, or more accurately *the* sexual energy is being raised. In truth the sexual energy or *Kundalini* is completely beyond the personal, it rises up from the depths of the Earth itself and if our energy centers are open, it moves through the body arousing it as an instrument of creativity, of giving and receiving sensation (pleasure), loving unconditionally.

Consider then that the 'fore-play' of the Old Paradigm becomes the process of 'raising one's energy', bringing in the God-force, welcoming the Goddess into your body, raising the *Kundalini* or Earth Energy or whichever words most speak to you. But the key point is that it is *trans-personal*, it is not '*my* sexuality', or '*my* sexual arousal' it is '*the* arousal of the *Kundalini*'.

There may be a tendency for those on the spiritual path to try to avoid the whole affair of the physical, which perhaps seems too 'gross'. Wishing to go straight into Spirit, into meditation and somehow make love from the 'lofty heights' of Spirit, bypassing the body as much as possible but this is likely avoidance, repression and aversion. You have got to release all that's in the box to reach the Light. Where there is attraction or aversion there is pain and we want not to run from it but to feel it so that we can reclaim ourselves. So we must go through the body, we cannot avoid the physical aspect of love-making, the sensuality of it, the pleasure of it.

Eventually once all attraction and aversion has been neutralized we may arrive at a joyful state of surrender to exist, embodying our natural equanimity. At this point, we are so in tune with ourselves and the *Kundalini* energy that its arousal happens more instantaneously and in a more subtle way as the energy centers open. The arousal of the energy may, for example, take no more than a gentle stroking of the feet and legs by our Beloved, encouraging the natural flow as it moves freely around the body.

Again we do not want to run from pleasure, this natural gift of the physical experience, but neither do we want to run towards it, lest we deny ourselves the ecstatic communion and union with the Cosmic

Beloved, which is the goal of the *yogi/yogini* and the true purpose of love-making as a trans-personal vehicle for those seeking deeper connection to the Mystery of Life.

The first time I Maha entered the vibration of that which is beyond pleasure/pain and discovered this cosmic treasure it was like this:

In the *yoni*[12] was pain. Perhaps the stored accumulation of making-love unconsciously. Perhaps it was the stored ignominy of many life-times, or the collective memory of female pain-body identification; of agonizing child-birth, of rape, abuse, dis-respect and misunderstanding as well as mental projections both self-inflicted and societal, all stored away in the cellular memory of the *yoni's* sensitive and intelligent tissue.

What was causing me the suffering so many times I made love was the *thought* to which I was fully identified 'I *should* be experiencing pleasure in my *yoni*' but instead, oftentimes there was pain and my thought, 'I *should* be experiencing pleasure in my *yoni*' was in itself resistance to the sensation. I had resistance to the

---

[12] The vulva/vagina (Sanskrit), a symbol of divine procreative energy (Divine Feminine, Creative Force).

whole experience because I was identified with my sexual pain-body.

Then I was guided etherically, held in the embrace of Presence, to go deeply into the pain sensations and drop the story. This degree of total surrender was not easy; it was a radical turning of the tides, a switching of deep, *karmic* patterning and a leap of faith. In this surrender, my beingness entered into a new *bhava*; I experienced myself as *Kali*, the destroyer of ego. Entirely holding the Presence of the witness state, my tongue stuck out, my eyes widened, and I hissed and snarled. Tears of emotional pain became euphoric laughter. I was loving the pain with so much freedom that I (this was a state far beyond the level of the personality) slipped into a state of God-absorption, a state entirely beyond fear, a state of inner-knowing (a feeling, an experience, a realization) that there was ultimately no-thing whatsoever in existence to be afraid of.

What I experienced was a state-of-being that was far beyond any identification with form or having any preference over pleasure or pain. Instead, sensations of pain or pleasure trickled through my experience like a little stream far below. There was a feeling of total invulnerability, the *gnowing* that neither pain nor death could ever kill or harm this eternal source of Life at the root of me... at the root of all.

What we want is to be empowered in Spirit. In love-making, energy can be raised through mutual worship of the exquisite sensitivity of the human body, coming profoundly into the micro-moment, exploring one another's forms using all of the senses. Every area of our body is a possible gateway to the arousal of exquisite pleasure and... of the Eternal Spirit. Let us be absolutely clear, the acceptance of sensation (whatever Is) takes us into higher states of consciousness, into Spirit. If we become attached to the pleasure, we miss out on the higher purpose of love-making. But enjoy it, explore it, play in it, never judge what transpires and be open to transcending it.

Coming profoundly into the present moment, arousing one another's energy in this way becomes a meditation; each touch from your partner is from the Cosmic Beloved, each area of skin, a divine creation. Give yourself permission to arouse your own energy also (with or without your partner) treat it as a meditation and become accustomed to the way the energy flows around your own body.

This is not an 'act', a show for some other's bemusement, this is a blossoming of a truth. If resistance arises to being this sexual or physical, this aversion is something also to be explored.

For we must not be repelled or repulsed by the sensuality of form and of being in form, learning to love the body and all that it has to offer. For how can we be truly liberated whilst we hold resistance to part of the divine creation, indeed the very divine vehicle built to house and express our unique emanation of Spirit?

It is worth reminding ourselves that the I AM Presence is both masculine *and* feminine not male *or* female. Be open, in your *sadhana* to the experience of yourself beyond gender. Then you will realize just how much is bound up with the filter of being a woman or a man. And how freeing it is to transcend this narrowing!

The exploration of one another's bodies is the journey of enjoying the rich experience given to us in these forms and appreciating all of our senses and celebrating the exquisite sensitivity the Human Being is equipped with.

For instance, we may be attracted to the scent of the aroused *yoni* but there may be a confusion of thoughts and images and memories intermingled with pornographic imagery flooding the mind, or we may be repelled by it but either way, can we allow ourselves to drop all story around it and *open* to it and be Present completely to the vibration of it in the moment? In that scent, in fact, there is a subtle energy and if consciously experienced without attraction or aversion one can be lifted into the high vibration the *yoni* holds. It is worth remembering and exploring the truth that every area of the Human body is innocent; if feelings of rejection arise towards a certain part of your or your partner's body, then you could try looking at the area with a deep Presence through the eyes of your Heart.

So much has been projected upon the genitals and breasts in the Old Paradigm. The *lingum*[13] has long been characterized as, and used as, a 'weapon', intruding upon the *yoni*; an instrument of rape and lust but the *lingum* itself is completely innocent of these harsh projections and usages. It only exists to give Love; it is

---

[13] The penis (Sanskrit). A symbol of divine generative energy (Divine Masculine, Pure Consciousness).

built out of Love, it knows only Love, and if we tune into the subtle energy of it during love-making we may feel this truth most profoundly. The woman gives Love through the Heart, through the breasts and receives Love through the *yoni*. It is a cycle of giving and receiving Love between two forms in which personal identity can fall away, revealing the Truth.

All of our desires and aversions will ultimately want to see the Light. To go into these places, we will need our full awareness and a partner who is able to hold the space of non-judgment, surrender to Spirit, and bring a sense of play along with Unconditional Love. They are not something to be ashamed of but something to be interested by. For parts of us will need to be recovered from the hidden places within ourselves, those places to which we have been afraid to shine the light of our own consciousness.

We might be concerned that if we explore a certain fantasy that we will get absorbed in that fantasy and be putting on layers instead of removing them. Fantasies contain a degree of rejection, abstraction, and projection and so they are built out of pain. So there is a root cause of the fantasy, (perhaps an early experience that contained both feelings of arousal and feelings of embarrassment, shame or confusion) and mere repression of it will not be enough to reclaim yourself from it, in fact it will only fuel the fantasy and make it more 'hot'. You must *empower* yourself in the fantasy and this goes for exploring aversions also.

To rediscover your Self as Spirit is to realize nothing is more powerful.

Empowering yourself in the fantasy/aversion means going into the higher dimensions and playing in a judgment-free (safe), blameless zone. Nothing in a fantasy/aversion needs to be personal, instead when in this deep work, play in/surrender to archetypes. For instance, in exploring a Freudian fantasy we are not playing the role of our partner's mother on the level of form but instead we enter the vibration of the Divine Mother who is unconditionally loving, all embracing, and mother to all. This sets the stage to explore the deeper, impersonal roots of the fantasy for healing and unity.

Ultimately, we want to enter the part of our Self that is often referred to as the Witness. The part of us that is in Acceptance of every part of us; so that the totality of ourselves becomes our ally. In this way, we can enjoy everything but be identified with no-thing. We can become our True Self by not being resistant to our false selves, which are in and of themselves born out of resistance.

We say 'play in archetypes' that it might be a pointer to enter more deeply and fully into Presence together, without chasing, resisting or trapping us further in story, isolation and separation. As we explore and heal our inner realms, particularly when we play in archetypes, it can begin to feel as though we are healing parts of the whole of humanity, beyond even the experience of our own lifetimes, and *indeed this may well be the case.*

Let there be no shame of what passes through one's psyche, all identity must ultimately be un-dammed and allowed to pass through so as to reclaim the easy, guilt-free flow of Life, power, and purity, which are One.

Most important in love-making is that it builds Love between you, not lust. Lust is born out of imbalance, a strong attraction/aversion to the physical body as a sexual object. Love, on the other hand, is the feeling of your own blissful nature radiating from within you, taking you beyond the physical and into harmony with Life.

TRANSCENDING THE PERSONAL

The relationship that you have with your partner on the Esoteric Path of Marriage is the relationship that you have with your Self, the relationship that you have with God... eventually there is no separateness between me and God or me and my partner or between my partner and God.

The layers of separation come down one at a time. Unity begins when a 'cosmic gust of wind' (metaphorically speaking) sweeps in one moment and blows them all away, and gazing in to 'your partner's' eyes there is only God. Tears spring from the well in your Heart. You are looking into the eyes of the Creator, the Great Teacher itself, the living Presence behind all things! Feeling into the fathomless depth of Heart within. The Voice of Eternity is speaking to you from your partner's very mouth! The Cosmic Beloved, appreciating you as its perfect creation, as you were always 'meant' to be appreciated, a unique expression of its infinite nature, all beyond the limitations of the logic of the conditioned mind.

Your Beloved is in turn your holy father, your divine mother, your daughter and your son. This miracle happens in the space of the Heart far, far beyond identity. The depths of the Love, the Peace, the Joy, the Bliss, the Beauty, and the Intelligence of this Eternal Being cannot be conveyed in words... Then the layers blow back in again but the insights have been had, the Truth has been revealed and experienced and there is no going back.

Eventually, the cosmic wind blows away the final layer of separation and in experiencing God in your partner an absolute *me-ness* is revealed.

One has surrendered to deepest Devotion, the other is surrendering to the experience of completely dissolving the other until there is a merging of the outer and the inner; a profound Unity. allowing us to glimpse the Beauty-Love-Intelligence that is behind (and beyond) the scenes.

These moments of direct knowledge of the truth get longer and longer with progressively shorter intervals between them. Duality thus becomes a *play of consciousness*[14]. In this way the path of *bhakti* (devotion) that can be experienced between the Cosmic Beloved and devotee - sometimes played out between

---

[14] The phrase Play of Consciousness used here and page 186 is also the name of an autobiography by Swami Muktananda.

Guru and disciple, or between devotee and a particular form of God - are played out exquisitely within a marriage! Though it happens in form, it is experienced on the etheric levels of reality, far beyond the reaches of personality. It is a slow, unfolding of revelatory experience that cannot be forced. Coming into the rhythm of *Kairos* (God-Time) is a key. Ceasing to look for salvation and fulfillment on the outside of yourself is another.

At this point, there may be little time for the world. Hours and hours every day may be spent deep in revelatory experience (together) and time, mind and worldliness cease to exist for you. You may be seen to have retreated into your own little world, but there is nothing small about this expansive state of Unity.

(Whatever unfolds for you or your partnership on your Hero's Journey[15], remember you are Love and will be taken care of, by Love, one way or another and put in places and situations where you can deepen and be of benefit, emerging with an expanded perspective and a readiness to use your deepest gifts to benefit humanity.)

---

[15] Part of a philosophy at the heart of the teachings of Joseph Campbell.

During such a period for us, when for many months we dwelt in blissful, unified states of higher learning, we only emerged for a part-time job taking care of a young, disabled, non-verbal mystic. Such a job during such a period can only be magicked up out of the Mystery itself!

Intermittently during such periods, (for the sake of balance it should be mentioned,) our pain-bodies would clash. As the layers are being stripped away pain-bodies will feel themselves to be fighting for survival, so try to accept what arises without identifying too much in their drama and rejoice as over time the pain-body clashes become fewer and fewer, and further apart, and shorter in length.

From a shared state of Ecstasy and Bliss, beyond thought, out of the collective space that can be held by two, highly esoteric, mystical experiences and new states of consciousness can emerge. In our deep meditations together Divine *bhavas* have arisen and the teachings that have come have contributed immensely to the teachings in this book. More on these *bhavas* will be shared in future works.

As each of us is blessed with our own unique qualities, each will be blessed with their own unique experiences, expressions and states of consciousness as we transcend the personal and journey to Union with the source of Life itself! Most important is to stay equanimous and...

"Be the scientist of your own experience."

- Goenka

The survival of the Old Paradigm relies on its citizens staying asleep, therefore there is no such thing as Enlightenment or Self-Realization in the Old Paradigm. But the New Paradigm holds the space for each of us to become Awake with permission to be ever-expanding, evolving and free to be our Selves, forever-young and Eternal.

Awakening is a process of holding space for your deepest feelings and sensations (Your Truths) over and over again, dying to all that never was really you. All that is temporary and illusory and passing through, rocketing us through the apparition of Time. No problem to enjoy the experiences whilst they Are but if you hold onto them for even a second too long, they will cross over into shadow and you will miss the Joy,

Magic, Mystery and Divinity of all that is New, just like you.

May your relationships be a blessing to yourselves and everyone.

Our Hearts are connected from here on out and Always.

ACKNOWLEDGEMENTS

So many radiant lights both 'in body' and 'out-of-body', both knowingly and un-knowingly, directly and indirectly have contributed to this work. Here, we'd like to express gratitude to some of our Big Loves along the way: To Asha and Shirdi Sai Baba for your exquisite high company. To Joseph Campbell for reminding us of the importance of closing the loop. To Amma the Hugging Saint for being our Guru, marrying us and showering us with Love. Goenka for guiding us In; even if lying down. Dr. Michael Bernard Beckwith for uplifting and inspiring us and allowing us to imbibe your understanding regarding the Old and New Paradigm, which has been invaluable to the expression of this book. Also for your teachings on

Abundance Consciousness, which have so impacted our lives. To Karl Renz for always meditating. Eckhart Tolle for letting us know we had treasure within and inviting us to examine our minds. To the visionary Jana Dixon for teaching us to support Kundalini Awakening through super-nutrition. Dr Shakti Malan for following your intuition all the way to the Himalayas to open up our minds to Tantra. "You never know what something is for." – *A Course in Miracles*. Byron Katie for being a beacon of Beauty and Wisdom. To Marianne Williamson for blessing us with just a glance. To Don Miguel Ruiz for *The Mastery of Love*. Bob Dylan for being exemplary. Jan Vanek for being One with Music. To Joan of Arc for your Faith. And Jesus (Yeshua) for your examples of sacrifice and surrender.

BIG THANKS:

To the kind and generous Hearts who've reached out to catch us along the way as we've fallen through the cracks of the matrix to more certain ground within ourselves. Barbara and Tom, Baba and Emelina Flores, Isaac Mullins, Adrian Gans, Victor and Matt, Frances and the Lost Boys.

To Jane of Amritapuri for your Heart of Gold.

To Lyria for your powerful and compassionate Heart.

To Chandra for being one of the most unique and other-worldly Beings we've had the good fortune to come across, and for many meditations in our car.

John Raatz for excellent publishing advice. And to Alex Piner for technical support.

GLOSSARY

Ashram	A hermitage, monastic community, or other place of religious retreat
Ayurveda	The Ancient 'Life Science' of India
Bhakti	Devotion to the Eternal Presence
Bhava	A divine mood manifesting spontaneously from a high state of consciousness
Gnow/Gnowing	An effortless state of absolute inner-knowing, originating in the Heart
Japa	The practice of silently repeating a

mantra on the inside

Kali	An aspect of the divine Self that destroys ignorance and dispel darkness (ego). In ancient traditions she is depicted as a black-skinned Goddess with a protruding tongue and bulging eyes, bedecked with a necklace of human heads (representing ego).
Karma	Action or accumulation of action (from the ego as opposed to the non-action of the Witness State).
Kosmos	The entire Universe as a cohesive whole, which includes its subtle or etheric dimensions as opposed to the word 'Cosmos' which refers solely to the physical reality.
Kundalini	The feminine God-force; the Creative force behind Nature that lies latent within every Human Being for the purposes of evolution. Said to rise up the spine in a double helix of life-force.
Lingum	The penis (Sanskrit). A symbol of divine generative energy (Divine

Masculine, Pure Consciousness)

Mantra	A high vibrational set of syllables or invocation
New Paradigm	An elevated, subtle vibration 'within' (or a state of consciousness) that is beyond fear, worry, doubt and not-enough-ness
Old Paradigm	Man's struggle to survive as an isolated entity in an environment of scarcity and strife
Pancha Karma	The purification therapy used in Ayurvedic medicine. The word panchakarma means five actions and refers to five procedures intended to intensively cleanse and restore balance to the body, mind, and emotions.
The Presence	The One Eternal Consciousness that gives rise to everything; also called God, the Self, the Substratum etc
Sadhana	A Sanskrit word, literally meaning "method for receiving attainments". A sadhana is a practice that is a

method for attaining spiritual realizations.

Vasanas	Inherited tendencies

Vedic Astrology   Called "Jyotish" (Sanskrit), or the science of light, it is a discipline, which predicts the events happening in human life and in the Universe on a time scale. It assumes the law of karma, which states that a human being lives and works within certain parameters created by actions performed in prior lifetimes. Through Spiritual practices and the practice of non-reaction (entering a non-judgmental Witness State), it is said much (if not all) of a person's 'negative' Karma can transcended.

Yoni   The vulva/vagina (Sanskrit), a symbol of divine procreative energy. (Divine Feminine)

We invite all of our beloved readers to:

Share your experience of *The Esoteric Path of Marriage* with other readers on Amazon, Goodreads etc.

Feel free to write to us with your questions or share your journey with us personally through email @:

mahaanddavid@gmail.com

Connect with us through our blog:

https://mahaanddavid.blogspot.com

'Like' our book page on Facebook:

https://www.facebook.com/esotericpathofmarriage

To register interest for upcoming 'singles' and 'couples' retreats please visit:

www.esotericpathofmarriage.com

Sacred Human Press

www.sacredhumanpress.com

CPSIA information can be obtained at www.ICGtesting.com
Printed in the USA
LVOW11s0156050516

486693LV00003B/209/P